The Mystery and Magic
of the Occult

The Mystery and Magic of the Occult

by

JOHN STEVENS KERR

FORTRESS PRESS

Philadelphia

To my wife, Joanne, and my children—
David, Kirsten and Sean—who keep my
feet on the ground and my head in the clouds.

Library of Congress Catalog Card Number 79–154486
ISBN 0–8006–0157–2

4331C74   Printed in the United States of America   1–157

CONTENTS

Preface

The resurgence of the occult in the midst of history's most scientific period is a phenomenon that amazes some, puzzles others—and thoroughly excites the thousands who have found a new dimension of spirituality, for good or evil, in these long discredited arts.

This book is not written by a believer in any of the occult arts, but I have met and talked with many people who are deeply immersed in this new kind of religion, and came away rather impressed. Beneath the enormously complex variety of occult arts, one can discern a quest, a need, even the vague outlines of an emerging religious view that has a good chance of becoming prominent in spiritual thinking in the next few years. In a small way, this book attempts to uncover the positive dynamics that lie beneath the turbulent surface of the occult.

Very soon, the established churches, as bearers of traditional Christianity, will have to come to terms with the occult. And the encounter of these forces in our day must be more irenic, more patient than in the past. Large numbers of Christians, especially young people, are already synthesizing their received faith with their newly recovered occult philosophies.

I want to thank the scores of people who gave me so much time in interviews and who openly shared their thinking with me. I hope that where my point of view runs contrary to theirs, I have not caricatured their beliefs. It is, frankly, impossible for an outsider to write about the occult without sounding absurd to one who is immersed in it. Even though I am an outsider, I hope I have been open enough to sense the important positive (in my opinion) stream of truth that the banks of the occult enclose.

JOHN STEVENS KERR

Old Ideas Never Die—They Just Wait Their Time

The line between the natural and the supernatural blurs in our day. Supernatural refers to an order of existence beyond the observable visible universe. In popular usage, it has come to mean that which cannot be empirically validated, tested with the five senses. The natural domain belonged to scientific man; it could be tested, observed, proven, perhaps controlled. All that lay beyond this belonged to the supernatural; it was religion, magic, mystery, but not science. The natural world was the "real" world, and sensible people confined their life to this dimension, except for emotional excursions now and then into such fields as religion.

Such a view of the world no longer satisfies large numbers of people. They have a deep conviction, or feeling, that the "real" world contains phenomena and potentialities that go beyond the "visible and observable." Right or wrong, this view represents a shift away from total confidence in the rigorously scientific view of reality. This mental stance toward reality, this emerging world view that is more accepting of the "supernatural," makes the present revival of occult interest possible among educated people.

As human beings shift their attention from the outer world to themselves, from external nature to internal human nature, they open up to emotions, feelings, and long suppressed longings. They become much more patient with the "supernatural" because they discover that inside every man there is a certain quality—call it poetic, or religious, or a desire for a harmony of man and his world—that forever calls man to transcend himself. The transcendental world of thought and feeling takes on new importance.

We are at just such a time. We open up to the occult as we realize that it has been a part of human experience longer than science. It was, in fact, man's first science, in the sense that it represented our first human efforts to come to terms with nature. The divorce between man and his world, in which we assume that we can pull away from our ecological and symbiotic ties with the material world and examine it in total detachment, arose in the eighteenth century. Man's belief that thought can be detached from the self and therefore find truly objective truth is that recent. This attitude is actually a new interloper into our mental processes compared with the aeons of human history in which man operated more wholistically. When one feels that the purely rational view of man has run its course, as many do today, he turns once again to world views that synthesize the now separated spheres of thought and nature. Occultism had done, and continues to do, just that.

The word occult has four meanings in *Webster's Seventh Collegiate Dictionary*. The first three are somewhat related: the occult has to do with not revealed, secret things; with abstruse and mysterious things; and with those elements of experience which cannot be seen or detected, the concealed world. The word is also used to refer to supernatural agencies, their effects, and our knowledge of them. We use the word occult to refer to anything which we cannot explore in orthodox ways.

What religious types of experience we deem occult depends on which kinds of experiences the established, culturally accepted religions offer. When Christianity speaks of transforming one's life through an experience with Jesus Christ as the revealed and risen Lord and Son of God, we call this a religious insight. If someone in our culture spoke of life-transformation through identification with the Illuminated Seventh-Astral Aura, who is the Ultimate Revelation of the Cosmic Force and who holds sway over the

First through Ninth States of Being, we would say he dabbled in the occult. The form of each statement is the same; Jesus is simply a more orthodox and acceptable source of mystical experience than the Illuminated Seventh-Astral Aura. The average citizen who wanted to discuss religio-mystical experiences would feel more comfortable using "Jesus-talk" than "Aura-talk." What we call "religious" and what we call "occult" depends heavily on culturally conditioned uses of language.

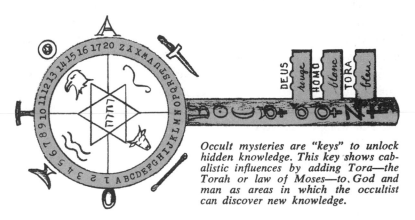

Occult mysteries are "keys" to unlock hidden knowledge. This key shows cabalistic influences by adding Tora—the Torah or law of Moses—to God and man as areas in which the occultist can discover new knowledge.

Speaking of the occult, then, causes us some difficulty. The word itself seems loaded with negative connotations and sounds a trifle unrespectable to our ears. It has come to embrace more or less magical experiences which do not fit into our usual acceptable categories.

Nevertheless, the kinds of experiences we label occult belong to most people in some form. One of the charms the occult holds for us is that we all have experiences that go a little beyond our abilities to explain them.

Here are a few such experiences people shared with me in various interviews:

A middle-aged woman said, "On that particular day, I felt very disturbed. I couldn't concentrate on my housework. It was as if my mind was off somewhere, only it wasn't a pleasant place. A kind of dread gripped me and it grew more intense as the day went on. Toward afternoon, the sense of danger became more focused. I thought of Tom, my son at college. I just knew he was in trouble or injured. Suddenly, a picture of an automobile accident flashed across my mind. I knew then that Tom had been hurt in a car accident. I went to the phone to call the college because I had to find out if I was right. Almost the very moment I reached the telephone, it rang. It was the college telling me that Tom had been injured in an accident and that he was in the hospital." This woman has no formal interest in psychic phenomena. As far as I know, she has never read any literature on the subject, and after this experience she did not turn to the occult. She simply had a "strange premonition." She wonders about it, is amazed with it, but she is content to let it rest.

A young accountant told me, "I was walking back to my office from lunch. I passed by the offices of (a major oil company). I had been very happy on my job and really hadn't thought of leaving. But when I strolled by this other company, a sudden impulse grabbed me. I had to go in. I remember that when I stood in the lobby, waiting for the elevator to take me to their floor, I felt like I was in a dream. I ordinarily don't go in for impulses, and this somehow didn't seem like me. Anyway, I spoke with their personnel people and it turned out they were looking for a man with my qualifications. I ended up taking a new job with them at a better salary and with a much better future. It was the best lunch hour I ever spent."

Many people told me of premonitions and flashes of intuition. You can collect your own data by listening to your friends. In several instances, the great insights weren't so great. The person who told me that when his phone rang one night, he knew it was news of his grandmother's passing had logical reasons for such a conclusion. His grandmother had been in intensive care for some time and the call came at 4:00 A.M. But other incidents such as the two described above seem quite out of character for the persons involved and don't seem to be logical outgrowths of any facts or continuing events. Such momentary, even isolated, psychic experiences are quite common.

Another kind of occult experience that involves huge numbers of people relates to divination, or predicting the future. Have you

4

heard stories that begin, "I knew it was a bad day when I woke up and fell out of bed . . ."? One man told me of a trip he and his family took which ended in a serious accident. He recounted the disasters that preceded it: lost car keys, a flat tire in the driveway, having to come back for an important piece of luggage, and so forth. He concluded, "We should have known it wasn't in the cards to take that trip. Someone somewhere was trying to tell us something."

Most of us have sensed the disquieting feeling while in a new place that "we have been here before." Usually it is a diffuse feeling, but sometimes it is remarkably vivid. One woman told me of her first visit to her future mother-in-law's farmhouse in Nebraska. This woman grew up in Seattle, had never seen a midwestern farm, yet she says that when she walked into the farmhouse she felt as if she even knew what was in each closet. As it turned out, she did. Some of these experiences might be explained as a surging forth of our unconscious. Images we have stored away through reading, or hearing stories, or seeing films, or talking with people, suddenly combine in new ways and emerge to surprise us. We have the impression that we have lived this scene before. On my first visit to New York City, I felt amazingly comfortable and at ease. I felt that I had been here before. Naturally, this experience had an obvious explanation. New York is a national city; through films and books and television, we all live there vicariously. Its landmarks, street names, people, and mood become part of our unconscious mind, and this surfaces when we come to the city. But some experiences of this nature aren't so easily explained. There may well be an explanation, but it is not easy. Since mystery and fact are relative terms, related to our capacity for making reasonable explanations, most of us find we have a large number of sensations and incidents in our lives that we are willing to label occult.

Tough-minded individuals refuse to concern themselves with any experience or issue that they cannot explain concretely on generally acceptable terms. If they can't explain something, they dismiss it from their minds. Other people allow themselves to wonder about the unexplained. They are more open to unorthodox interpretations of their experiences. The first group won't get involved with the occult or anything else romantic or poetic; the second group can and will enter into the intangible areas of feeling and intuition.

We should hesitate to say that one style of thought is "right" and the other is "wrong." We can profitably discuss which is more satisfying, more practical, more fruitful as a style of life, more enjoyable—but this is far different than saying one is on target and the other is way off. People tend to adopt a particular pattern of thinking because it satisfies their needs; if their need is to heal the breach between thought and nature, to form a harmonious, poetic view of life, they cannot work within the framework of detached objective thought.

Therefore, the most useful approach toward understanding the occult and the people's interest in it, is not down the line of trying to discover whether or not occult phenomena are "true" by certain scientific canons or "false." The best understanding of occult comes when we try to grasp why people are interested in it and accept it. The psychological and sociological dimensions of the occult suggest more to us than the scientific aspects, or their provability. People will believe the most patently absurd and insane notions, if they want to believe them badly enough. The more fascinating question is, why do they want to? As we answer that question, we shall have an appreciative insight into the occult.

We have suggested that the current explosion of interest in the occult goes deeper than a mere fad. However, there are faddish aspects to it. The occult is "in," right now. We read about it, hear it in songs, see it in plays and films, listen to people discuss it on TV, buy it on greeting cards, see its symbols on the checks the bank gives us. Occult symbols, especially those belonging to astrology, constitute a pop art form, and their verbal equivalents afford us a convenient framework for cocktail party conversation. Fads come and fads go, but if the analysis is correct that several factors in modern culture have combined to provide a fertile ground for occultism, we can expect the dark and hidden mysteries to be around for some time. The religio-philosophical mood of the next decade may well find itself shaped by basically occult ideas.

One can find at least four reasons why the occult has survived since its birth in the dawn of history. It made it through the period of scientific domination, it withstood the onslaughts of reason well enough to appear full-dress in the advanced and sophisticated seventies. The occult seems to fill some basic desires of man.

The first is man's desire to predict the future. The occult began in the dim reaches of civilization as a predictive methodology. The Babylonians used astrology to predict weather; other cultures used psychic prophets or divination techniques to predict the outcome of battles or the future of a ruling dynasty. In this sense, the occult was man's first science, because the goal of science is to be able to predict events. A scientific theory becomes a "law" to the degree that it can accurately predict what will happen, given certain circumstances. Our favorite predictive device today is statistical projection. From an analysis of past events, we are able mathematically to predict how future trends will go. In the long run, these kinds of predictions have validity. That is, they tend to be accurate. In the short term, such as telling us what will happen to us tomorrow, they don't have anything to say. When it comes to predicting hundreds and thousands of years ahead, the statistical methods collapse completely.

So, people who want some clues as to what might befall them in the next few days, or who wish guidance about the fate of the planet or civilization over the next few millennia, must turn to other sources. Occult techniques of dream interpretation, astrological calculation or divination offer some means to probe the immediate future. It doesn't matter if these techniques are based on logical or reliable premises. There is nothing better and the occult approach comforts an individual by giving him something to supplement his own intuition. Many of us are prisoners of the scientific approach to the extent that we distrust pure intuition. We need some operation, some methodology to supplement it. Horoscope casting, or reading cards is a complex methodology that provides support for our insecurities about our own guesses.

Projections into the distant future have never been a province of science. Certain historical theories, such as the cyclical theories that history repeats itself, may appear under such impressive authorship as the brilliant Arnold Toynbee, but they amount to little more than intelligent guesswork. One simply cannot find hard-core facts to prove reliably that the fate of the United States or Western Europe can be derived from a close study of the decline of the Roman Empire. While the projections of noted historians may be more acceptable than the predictions of a golden Age of Aquarius coming from an astrologer, neither one is more

The zodiac signs are often arranged in a circle, a left-over idea from the Ptolemaic view of the solar system.

coldly scientific than the other. Even historiography shades into the occult. Classic Christianity offers a long-term prediction about the future of human life. Its doctrine about Jesus Christ coming again "to judge both the quick and the dead" is an apocalyptic vision of the end of history which differs in words—not substance —from occult theories about the future of mankind.

So long as people want to know what will happen tomorrow, they are open to the occult, whether it is clearly labeled as such (by listening to Jeane Dixon's psychic interpretations of the future) or hidden under other names (such as following political

8

pundits in the press, or accepting the predictions of a learned re-searcher—both of whom may generalize and make intuitive predictions far beyond what their factual data will support).

The second appeal of the occult seems to explain quickly the whole movement: The occult satisfies neurotics. People who don't like the occult often dismiss it as a floating funny farm inhabited by disturbed males, and those females who failed to achieve a complete transition through menopause. When you attend meetings of some older occult groups, such as the Theosophical Society of America, you mingle with a better than middle-aged crowd who seem weirder than a normal collection of people. If you attend classes on aspects of the occult that have recently sprung up all over the country, you meet a different crowd. They are younger, brighter, and generally more normal. Women seem to predominate, and if they have any hang-ups, they are the same ones shared by many intellectual young women: a deep need to be involved in a cause or a meaningful quest. Any bald statement that all occult devotees are neurotic simply goes far beyond acceptable limits. Some occult fans are nuttier than the proverbial fruitcake, others are as normal as Mom's highly touted apple pie. Anyone with wide experience in religious circles knows too well that classic Christianity, and its spin-off sects, also mothers a lot of neurotics.

While it is true enough that neurotics and the occult can easily get together, we cannot lightly dismiss the occult as a haven for the disturbed. Instead of being surprised that a few such people latch onto the occult, we should be noticing the large numbers of intelligent, rational, obviously "normal" types that follow these movements.

The third, and much more important, appeal of the occult is the way it satisfies our desire for gnosticism. Gnosticism deals with "higher knowledge." It is usually hidden knowledge and open only to the initiates who penetrate the mysteries through discipline and study. All of us like to know something the other guy doesn't. We enjoy the "eenee, meenie, miney, moe, I know something you don't know" game. Freemasonry uses it well and most of the occult and mystical movements in our time rely on this basically snobbish attitude that human beings hold dear.

Some people need to be snobs in their ideas as well as their tastes and habits; they want to be one-up on the masses in all departments of life. But other people simply are not helped by currently popular religious and political myths. They are the kind who must "work out their own salvation" and cannot find complete satisfaction in adopting secondhand any of the available ready-made systems of belief. Such people prefer the hard work of tailor-making their own religious and philosophical ideas to picking them up off the rack.

Individuals who work within the Judeo-Christian tradition often adapt the beliefs of their sect to their own personality. A survey of the typical Christian congregation might reveal an embarrassingly large number who put their own interpretation, their own "higher truth" on the straightforward statements of the Apostles' Creed. These people find they fight a battle against prevailing orthodoxy and usually decide to keep their personal theology to themselves. The one who openly "spiritualizes" the atonement doctrine in a Presbyterian, Catholic, or Lutheran church soon discovers he is suspect and his name is high on the "pastoral care" list. The occult has not yet solidified into a rigid orthodoxy; it is more open and exploratory. You can put bits and pieces of the various occultisms together into your own personal mix and no one is going to scream heresy.

People who for any reason can't find satisfaction in the orthodox creeds, yet want to be part of a basically religious and spiritual movement, find the occult is a pleasant place in which to work out their own world view. It provides fellowship, groups, ideas, and opinions to work with, but it doesn't cramp their personal style. Established freethinking religious groups, such as the Unitarians and Ethical Culture Societies, are quite cerebral. They attract the intellectual person, while the emotionally inclined individual might seek his spiritual future in the congenial, religiously flavored atmosphere of the occult.

Finally, there is that large and growing number of people who move into the occult for positive reasons. They feel that it is a serious and valid alternative, a promising pathway to religious and spiritual insights that meets the needs of our time. This seems like

10

an amazing statement to make in the seventies, in the atomic era, in the time when man is reaching out to the moon and beyond. But it is absolutely true. I have spoken to scores of people who are in the occult not because they want to know the future, not for neurotic solace, not trying to be a snob, but because they are deadly serious about framing a personal faith through the maze of the occult. They want a religious experience that the established faiths cannot, or will not, offer. The kind of faith they want to build may not end up looking like any of the traditional occult sciences, but it will bear their stamp. And it may well become a promising faith in the next decade. What the contours of this emerging religion might be is something we will go into later.

There are a number of aspects to the occult, a variety of activities that go on under the one label. They range from astrology to spiritualism, from psychic phenomena to clairvoyance, from divination to black magic. Some of these are likely to pass into obscurity after a brief time on center stage, but at least a few of the occult arts seem destined to survive our times and become a part of our religious and philosophical outlook. It is worthwhile to take a close look at the several types of occultism in order to check their history, their ideas, and their potential for the future needs of man. ≈

What's Written in the Stars?

Astrology holds honors as the most popular occult art. The new astrological vogue marched on stage accompanied by its own anthem, "Aquarius." This song exposed the mysterious alignment of the heavenly bodies and promised that this configuration would bring love and peace.

And so, in the midst of a tribal rock fest titled "Hair," the dawning of the Age of Aquarius[1] was announced. People who had never given a thought to astrology sang the song, felt the promise, and the horoscope rush was on. The hippies, with love beads on their necks and astral symbols on their minds, set the Aquarian mood. Avant-garde favorites helped encourage the boom with their obeisance to the stellar powers. Norman Mailer talked

---

1. The Age of Aquarius is a slippery term. Not all astrologers agree on its meaning. A common view holds that this golden age of humanity and compassion begins when the vernal equinox moves into the sign of Aquarius, which will happen about the end of this century. However, the vernal equinox will have shifted its location by then so that it will actually be in the constellation of Pisces. The astrological Piscean Age is the Christian era, which some say has already ended. So, there are astrologers who say the Age of Aquarius is upon us, while others say it is just around the corner. Carl Payne Tobey, an astrologer, says, "I don't think anyone knows for sure." The ancients divided history into 2000-year periods, each identified with one of the twelve zodiacal signs. This 24,000-year cycle is now related to the 26,000-year procession of the equinoxes (see below). The results are confusing. But the Age of Aquarius, whenever it comes, is a good period, astrologically speaking.

astrological politics when he observed that the 1968 Republican National Convention did well to choose Miami Beach as its headquarters. He was convinced that this tropical fairyland must be the most materialistic city in the country (which fact makes it, in his opinion, a natural site for GOP nominations). He explained his view simply. "It is said that people born under Taurus and Capricorn are the most materialistic of us all. Take a sample of the residents in the census of Miami Beach. Does Taurus predominate more than one-twelfth of its share? It must, or astrology is done. . . ." So far no one has checked out Miami Beach birthdates to see if Mailer was right or not.

But astrology, by its very nature, is something that doesn't need to be checked out, like a Boeing 707, before one deems it safe for a flight. Marshall McLuhan, famous for his *Understanding Media* in which he analyzes the impact of electronic media upon our "global village," accepts astrology as one of the media of the age in the way most people do—by intuitive conviction. "I *know* I'm a Moon child, born under Cancer," he is reported to have said. "I can feel it in my veins."

The fashion industry swims in astrology up to its buttons. The leading designers and fashion houses consult the stars carefully before making any move. Introducing a new collection under an inauspicious combination of stellar bodies is a thought which terrorizes the night dreams of noted designers. Movie and entertainment stars, of course, have long consulted astrologers, having sought what the stars say about stardom for years, but recently they find it is safe to admit it publicly. One artist's agent told me, "Opera singers, actors, show people—they are all nuts on astrology. This is such an insecure business, you look anywhere for a hint about your next contract."

J. P. Morgan, the great financier, is said to have consulted, back in the thirties, the great American mother of astrology, Evangeline Adams. He sought guidance for his investments. For him, this may have been a desperation move. After the Great Crash, *anyone's* guess made sense since the "experts" in the market missd the mark completely. But in the more tranquil market of today, investors still consult astrologers, and some investment advice bulletins draw all their hot tips from the stars.[2] In Los Angeles, a TV stock market program includes astrological market analysis.

There is no shortage of important (and quite ordinary) people who lean on astrological advice. To assist them, between 5,000 and 10,000 astrologers offer their services professionally. No one can determine the exact number, because the field has no professional standards. Anyone who wishes can hang out a shingle and go into practice. Most of these professionals work the home town trade at $5.00 to $10.00 a visit. In the cities, big names get more. The professional elite, especially those such as Carroll Righter, Sidney Omar and Jeane Dixon who have syndicated columns and published books, command handsome yearly earnings. Much as doctors used to bill their services, the astrologer's fee is intimately related to the client's ability to pay.

If you can't make it to an astrologer personally, the marvels of our technological age assist you with a computerized horoscope. You feed in the important data, and the machine reads out your horoscope. The charge usually runs $20.00 and department stores selling the service allow you to charge it. The readout is rather complete. The service operated by Time Pattern Research Institute programs an IBM 360 computer with nineteen million bits of astrological data. Your readout runs about ten thousand words and offers you a character analysis, a list of your special aptitudes, along with forecasts for the year ahead. One firm expanded on the computer concept. They charge a monthly fee and give you a phone number and a code number which tells the machine what astrological classification you belong in. If you need emergency help, any hour of the day or night, you dial the number and give your problem to the girl at the machine. She types in your question, feeds the machine your code number, then reads the instant analysis back to you—and all before your three minutes are up.

The ordinary astrological enthusiast relies on the collective horoscopes published in newspapers, magazines and books. These are so general that many professional astrologers consider them

2. Horoscopes can be erected for companies and organizations, using the founding data and time. Carroll Righter did a horoscope once for Strasenburgh Planetarium of Rochester, New York, as part of a program offered on astrology and astronomy.

worthless. Nevertheless, Carroll Righter, the dean of American astrologers and one who can do a thoroughly professional private horoscope, also syndicates a collective horoscope column without feeling he is doing a disservice to his art. These horoscope columns have enjoyed a rising popularity since their introduction in the twenties. *Editor and Publisher,* the trade journal of the newspaper business, estimates that 1,200 of the 1,750 dailies in the United States carry such columns. Add to this the weekly papers that run horoscope columns and one senses that Richard Lewinsohn's estimate of 2,000 papers may be low. In addition, about 20 magazines deal mainly with astrology. Large circulation monthlies, especially those geared to female readers such as *Seventeen* and *Bazaar,* offer astrological columns. (As with most occult arts, women interested in astrology outnumber men three to one.)

The tiny "purse books" that sell at drug and supermarket checkout counters are slanted to (female) mass audiences and represent a good barometer of the popular tastes. The Dell line is heavy on astrology and includes other occult arts, such as dream interpretation and numerology. Several publishers offer horoscope-for-the-year booklets. One market manager told me, "Those astrology books sell faster than *TV Guide.*"

If history and background make a science respectable, astrology belongs to Burke's Peerage. It is one of the oldest mathematical exercises and prescientific endeavors in the long history of man. As the long span of human history goes, astrology has enjoyed the support of popes and kings down to modern times. We all know that it eventually phased into the modern discipline of astronomy, but we often forget how recently that happened. The great astronomical pioneers of the sixteenth century, such as Tycho Brahe, still cast horoscopes for their bread and butter while pioneering the new science of astronomy. The patrons of stellar observation at that time were more interested in the influences of the planets on their reigns than they were in the exquisite abstract concepts which these early astronomers were developing as scientists.

The period of the Renaissance, in fact, was a blooming time for astrology. Pope Julius II called upon astrologers to choose a propitious time for his coronation. His successor, Leo X, an otherwise learned and skeptical man, surrounded himself with astrologers who firmly predicted a long and tranquil reign for His Holiness. Regrettably, their horoscopes failed to reveal that Luther's Ninety-five Theses were not simply the academic dabblings of a cloistered professor of theology.

Luther rejected astrology with vehemence, although not so much because of its fundamental differences with his view of evangelical Protestantism. Luther disliked it for the same reason he disliked a number of other things—the Vatican liked it. Luther's close friend and intellectual compatriot, Philipp Melanchthon, looked on astrology as a serious science, even though Philipp was quite a rationalist who distrusted all forms of superstition. The astrological issue during the Reformation cut across all parties, so one cannot say that Rome was pro-astrology while the Protestant leaders opposed it. Pope Paul III, the first pontiff of the Counter-Reformation, was faced with the delicate task of moving hard against the reformers. He called in all the help he could muster, including astrologers to choose the best time for his consistory.

Astrology begins in the dim recesses of history. Imagine for a moment that you are back in 3000 B.C. You are sitting on a mound somewhere in Mesopotamia between the Tigris and Euphrates Rivers one evening observing the starry vault above you. No one is around to tell you that the sun is the center of the solar system and other such modern ideas. You must rely on your common senses. What will you see?

You will see a dark dome over your head, neatly fitted around the obviously circular, flat earth. In this dome, you see bright points of light, immutable and fixed, forever remaining the constant elements in the vortex of life's changing experiences. We know these stars move over periods of millenniums or so, but within one lifetime they are essentially fixed. As you watch this dome of diamondlike sparkles, you notice that different stars appear overhead as the year goes through its cycle of seasons.

These stars become your friends. You begin to see some patterns in their arrangements and you give these arrangements names. The names are chosen from your mythology, because looking at the stars brings a mysterious feeling of wonder and these beautiful nocturnal companions must certainly associate with the divinities.

If you are particularly sharp-eyed, you notice that five of these stars move enough to enable you to notice their motion. You call them wanderers (planets). Two of them appear near sunrise and sunset, the morning and evening stars. One (our Venus) is very bright, a perfect jewel. The other (our Mercury) shifts from morning to evening star rapidly and appears only briefly before sunrise or after sunset. Three others move more slowly: the red, fiery wanderer (our Mars), the two bright and yellowish topazes (Jupiter and Saturn).

More obviously, you see a huge companion, the moon. It goes through phases on a regular cycle and you find you can measure the passage of time from one "dark" (new) moon to the next. Your wife has a wondrous occurrence, her menstrual flow, in the same cycle as the moon. The sun, of course, fills your days. You watch its shadows lengthen with the seasons, its zenith drop as the year progresses. Crops are planted and harvested in rhythm with the sun. There is a lot to observe in the heavenly vault; you notice it all and come to feel that this regularity of the celestial sphere —which seems absolutely reliable—must have a purpose, even a divine purpose.

You are now ready to give birth to primitive astrology. You are prepared to accept the fundamental premise of astrology, that there is a casual connection between the stars and human events.

The first Babylonian astrologers have suffered the fates of time; we have lost their records. We do, however, have texts traceable to 2000 B.C. and data to indicate that astrology began about 1000 years earlier. The Babylonians developed the initial concept of the Zodiac, which later figured so prominently in astrology. For them, the Zodiac was an afterthought. They considered that the "wild goats" (*bibbu,* our planets), rather than the more static and placid stars, exerted the major force on human life. Each was the seat of a divinity: four males, except for one, the brightest (Venus) which was the home of Ishtar Astarte, the goddess of sexuality and fertility.

Nevertheless, the Zodiac was a triumph of observation, considering that it was accomplished with the naked eye from the top of a ziggurat (such as the biblical Tower of Babel).

The Zodiac is an observational construct. First, one traces the apparent path of the sun through the stars, which requires some imagination, because you can't see the stars in the daytime. This path, which we call the ecliptic, is rather close to the paths of the five naked eye planets. So, by running imaginary lines about 8° either side of the ecliptic, one constructs an imaginary belt about 16° wide. The stars in this zodiacal belt do not form obvious patterns, but eventually the ancients discovered twelve such constellations. The number twelve was related to the twelve moon cycles (months) that comprise one circuit of the sun around its path (a year).

At first, Babylonians directed their astrological predictions toward figuring out the weather. They relied heavily upon the moon, because it represented their chief divinity, although we know it is the sun which, of all the heavenly bodies, most influences our weather. Later, their prophecies took a political turn as the rulers sought advice for battles and clues about the future of their dynasty in those turbulent years when thrones changed hands with each passing of a (poisoned) goblet. This shift to the influence of stars on specific human events marks the beginnings of the horoscope style of astrology we use today, and was finally developed by later Mesopotamians and Greeks into an elaborate art.

The Egyptians were given to incorporating mystifying elements into religion. The priests worked in darkness, they manipulated statues to make them move and amaze the masses. At Heliopolis, near modern Cairo, they developed a center for astrological prediction. They weren't interested in meteorology, because the rise and fall of the Nile controlled their crop planting, so they embellished the personally predictive parts of the art. Egyptians added a lot of mystery to astrology.

Meanwhile, history brought the skilled Greek mind to bear on the subject. The conquests of Alexander the Great carried astrological wisdom from Babylonia to Greece. Aristotle supported its basic ideas, and the Pythagorean myths, with the other mystery cults of the time, offered fertile ground for astrology to root in.

The Romans believed deeply in the stars; Shakespeare reminds us of this when he has the soothsayer hail Julius Caesar in the first act of his famous play by the same name. This man, an astrologer, comes before Caesar to tell him, "Beware of the Ides of March." Caesar dismisses the predictor with a word to Brutus, his eventual assassin: "He is a dreamer; let us leave him—." It was, of course, exactly on the Ides of March that Brutus slipped the fatal dagger into Caesar. This may only indicate that Shakespeare and his contemporaries were the real occult enthusiasts (as they were). However, we have a great deal of evidence to suggest that the Shakespearian Caesar's cavalier dismissal of the soothsayer as "a dreamer" was fairly uncommon skepticism in Roman times.

Lucretius (99–55 B.C.) Romanized the philosophical skepticism of Epicurius in his long poem, *On the Nature of Things*. The materialism of Epicurianism intrigued Lucretius because it promised salvation from fear, the fear of the powers of the heavens. So powerful was the spell of those who could divine the turn of events from heavenly stars that many Romans lived in trembling anxiety. The Epicurian maxim that nothing can be created out of nothing became for Lucretius a gospel of freedom:

> Our cornerstone—that ne'er, by power divine
> Doth aught rise out of nothing. For this fear
> Doth cramp all mortals with a cringing dread,
> Since they behold in earth and heaven appear
> Full many a sign whose inward cause their minds
> Can nowise grasp, and so would faith believe
> The source thereof to be a power divine.[3]

The astrological system we now have comes to us from the general period of the Roman Empire. Hipparchus, working in Mesopotamia about 150 B.C., conducted his stellar investigations in the curious mix of astrology and astronomy that would characterize the science for 1600 years. Hipparchus developed the system of classifying the stars according to brightness into six classes. We still use his groupings of stars into "magnitudes" of brightness. At the same time, he more fully developed the Zodiac as we now know it. He formulated the twelve houses (each segment of the Zodiac is called a house as a vestige of the thought that gods

3. Lucretius *On the Nature of Things* 1. 153–59.

domiciled in the heavenly bodies) and assigned them their identification with mythological figures.

Much of his work was incorporated by the extremely learned Alexandrian scholar, Claudius Ptolemy, whose monumental work *Tetrabiblios* (about A.D. 150) became the scriptures of astronomy until Copernicus in the sixteenth century put forth the present heliocentric view.

This earth-centered view predominated European thought until the sun-centered view of Copernicus triumphed, because the newer view explained more of the mounting collection of observable facts. The church, of course, opposed the Copernican revolution, presumably because the earth, as the locus of Christ's work, obviously had to be at the center of all that was. Actually, the first pope who heard the theory did not object to it. Only when the contradiction between the heliocentric view and the basic premises of astrology, which was then taught in universities as well as being a passion of powerful and learned men, became obvious did the church move seriously against Copernicus's innovations. The fact is, the church, and its leaders at the time, went for astrology.

The Ptolemaic system provided the fundamental theoretical scheme for astrology. First, it viewed the earth as the center of the universe. This is a convenient perspective for making claims that the total forces of the stellar universe concentrate exclusively upon man's destiny. Today we are less confident. We know that we are part of the Milky Way galaxy, which is only one of the countless galaxies we can view through telescopes, and the universe is really a collection of these self-contained star systems. All of the stars we see with our eyes belong to our home galaxy. We discovered the true magnitude of our universe only after the development of huge optical and radio telescopes. All this has happened in our century. Medieval men can be forgiven if their cosmic view was myopic.

Second, the Ptolemaic view puts the earth at the center of the planetary and solar motions. This suggests a pattern which lends credence to the notion that their movements can influence life on earth in a significant way. One's common sense surely supports this conception of things, for that is the way it looks. We often forget how carefully we have been trained by modern science, so that we no longer see things as they come to our eyes. The earth is "obviously" flat; to believe it is round requires a level of sophistication beyond that of the common observer. So it is with our view of the solar system. The sun, moon and planets "obviously" arch the earth. People couldn't shake loose from two ideas which kept Ptolemy's universe alive even when mounting observational evidence shook its foundations. One was that the earth had to be the center of it all. The second was a Grecian hangover that the circle was the perfect geometrical form, and being perfect it must be God's chosen form, and since God made the heavens all bodies in the skies must move in perfect circles—even if these circles had to be compounded to the point where one could hardly draw a legible diagram of their motions.

Science thrives on simple explanations of phenomena. When Copernicus postulated the sun as the center of the solar system, he offered an idea which quite simply explained all these confusing motions. Kepler later developed his basic laws of planetary motion based on elliptical instead of circular orbits. The whole complex scheme of epicycles was overthrown by adopting two new assumptions: the sun is the center of the solar system, and the planets don't move in circles. The resistance with which these clarifying ideas were met is a tribute to the tenacity of old ways of thought. Astrology, in a strong sense, is another testimony to man's unwillingness to change his thinking.

Astrologers therefore continue to base their calculations upon the description of the universe as laid down by Ptolemy. They have only incorporated a couple of new ideas into their system—specifically those planets invisible to the naked eye.

William Herschel discovered Uranus in 1781, Adams and Le Verrier located Neptune in 1846, and the American astronomer Clyde Tombaugh discovered Pluto in 1930. The five naked eye planets now had three companions. Astrologers have slipped Uranus and Neptune into their tables of planetary influences, but so far not too many bother about Pluto. This distant planet moves so slowly (loafing about the sun in just under two hundred fifty years) that it hardly shifts position over a period of two or three generations. Saturn, the farthest out of the naked eye planets, moves about the sun in just under thirty years. It moves one Zodiacal sign every two-and-a-half years. This gives it sufficient speed to make an apparent difference in its situation relative to other astral bodies within one generation. Astrology attempts to make character differentiations between people, even when they are born close to each other. Such ponderously slow planets as Neptune and Pluto are not very useful in this task. By the time they creep from one "house" on the Zodiac to the next, a whole generation can come to birth. Fast-moving planets such as Mercury, which scurries about the sun in eighty-eight days, and Venus, which makes a journey in two hundred twenty-four days, skip from "house" to "house" rapidly enough to be of astrological use.

Astrologers have done little with the minor planets or asteroids. The first of these, Ceres, was discovered on New Year's Day, 1801, by the Italian astronomer Piazzi. Something like two thousand of these objects have been catalogued to date. They run, sometimes in eccentric orbits, between Mars and Jupiter, ranging in size from Ceres' 437 miles in diameter down to perhaps 3 or 4 miles. There are simply too many of them to fit into astrological calculations, which are complex enough as it is. But the skeptic might raise the question that if Mars has influence in my life, why doesn't this host of varied planetoids also affect my destiny?

Modern astronomy reveals a motion of the earth which makes the whole apparatus of zodiacal signs rest upon an illusion. The earth wobbles like an expiring top, a phenomenon called the procession of the equinoxes.

If the north-south pole of the earth is projected out to the stars, it will trace a circle of about 47° diameter over a period of nearly 26,000 years. The earth, wobbling about its polar axis, thus causes the apparent position of the stars to shift. Right now, the star we call the North Pole Star is Polaris, in the Little Dipper. By the year 2100, variations of the earth's procession will move Polaris even closer to true north. In the year 14000 navigators can use the bright star Vega as their northerly guide, although it will be farther from true north than our present North Star. In the days of Egyptian and Mesopotamian civilization, the north point was very near the star Alpha Draconis, which is the reference point for such geometrically precise edifices as the pyramids.

This intriguing earthly motion would not affect astrology, except for the embarrassing fact that the procession of the equinoxes affects the position of the sun on a given day. When Ptolemy and Hipparchus did their work, the spring equinox (March 20–21) occurred when the sun was in the constellation Aries, the Ram. Right now, the sun is actually in the neighboring zodiacal constellation Pisces, the Fishes, on that date. Consequently, astrological charts call the person born March 21–April 19 an Aries. For anyone now living, that is wrong. The sun was really in Pisces on his birthday.

If astrologers suggest that the stars in which the sun happens to be when you are born can influence you, it would be logical to pick the right stars. The procession of the equinoxes would complicate that problem because the Zodiac is a mathematical concept which is valid from a terrestrial point of view at a given moment in time. Therefore, astrologers speak of "signs." They say the person born March 21–April 20 came into the world under the "sign" of Aries. The sign, or the signification and meaning, is more important than the actual constellation involved. Astrological signs are the constellations in which the sun moved in Ptolemy's day. They have no relationship to the actual position of the sun in our present era. The sun has now slipped back one constellation behind the astrological sign.

One may safely conclude that scientific premises for astrology do not exist. But astrology certainly does exist; it is alive and well and living in our midst. Whether it fits into our developing cosmology or not doesn't seen to distract its enthusiasts. The reason, of course, is that people do not follow astrology as a science, but more as a matter of faith. It is a symbol system, a religion if you will, that satisfies deeply felt needs.

The real essence of astrology lies in the way in which it manipulates symbols. We all enjoy symbols, picture language, signs and illustrations. They are warmer, as it were, than facts. We speak of "warm words" at the same time we say "cold facts." A fact is emotionally less involving than a symbol. Christian saints don't go into raptures over the factual biography of Jesus. Their enthusiasm goes out to symbols—such as Savior and Son of God—associated with Jesus, rather than to his established movements in ancient Palestine. The Crucifixion inspires Christian devotion because of the cluster of symbolic associations connected with it. Many thousands of ancients were crucified, but only one such event, that involving Jesus, has collected symbolic meanings. Religion, poetry, fiction, philosophy and other rich parts of our heritage depend totally on symbols. Man is not yet a completely scientific animal.

The symbol system of astrology draws upon Greek mythology and the various influences given to sun signs and planetary influences derive from the characteristics of their mythological namesakes. If the ancients gave other names to the constellations and planets, astrologers today would be writing different horoscopes.

The basic element in their symbol system is the Sun sign. Using the placement of the sun as it was 2000 years ago, they present a series of signs of the Zodiac, beginning with the sign that opens spring—the season of planting, new life, and fertility. In addition, the ancients perceived four elements, Earth, Air, Fire, and Water, which held great significance for them. This fourfold symbol was worked into the twelvefold symbol system of the Zodiac. A common scheme of classifying human nature—as active, stable, and variable—also found its way into the Sun sign scheme. By mixing so many variables together, the astrologer increases his possible combinations. This increases his chances for pegging at least some characteristics you might have.

Though astrologers differ somewhat, this is the way the system more or less works out:

Number of "House"	Sign Name	Translation	Ruling Planet	Dates	Characteristics	Controls this part of body
I	Aries	the Ram	Jupiter Mars	March 21– April 19	Sun at spring comes alive again, a peak moment for the sun. Fiery, brilliant. Rams are daring, adventurous. Negative sides of this sign include characteristics associated with sheep: easily led, placid, etc.	Head and face
II	Taurus	the Bull	Venus	April 20– May 20	Like a bull: stubborn, strong, good health sign. Stormy love affairs; conservative, practical mind. Plodding, like an ox.	Throat, ears, jaw
III	Gemini	the Twins	Mercury	May 21– June 20	Based on symbolic implications of twins: changeable, double lives, variety. Negatively, leaves things half-finished.	Arms, hands, shoulders, respiratory tract

IV	Cancer (called Moon children since Cancer became associated with a dread disease)	the Crab	Moon	June 21–July 22	Crabs suggest lassitude, and also tenacity. Since crabs are hard to psyche out, Cancer people are said to fall into active and passive types. Called a "water" sign, and this is considered weak, having characteristics of "watery" people.	Breasts, stomach
V	Leo	the Lion	Sun	July 23–Aug. 22	What else for a lion, but strength, ambition, mastery. A powerful sign, the "king of human beasts" worthy of being "lionized."	Spine, back, heart
VI	Virgo	the Virgin	Mercury	Aug. 23–Sept. 22	Called an earth sign, it gets "earthy" and "down to earth" characteristics. Like we might surmise of vir-	Small intestines, abdominal cavity

VII	Libra	the Scales	Venus	Sept. 23–Oct. 22	gins, Virgo people are retiring, discriminating, a bit unapproachable. Bright, but uncreative. Cool, eventempered, as one who has not experienced the passions of lovemaking might be symbolically represented.	Kidneys, lower back

As scales symbolize justice today, the Libra is said to weigh things carefully, balance issues, and be just. Excellent judgment.

| VIII | Scorpio | the Scorpion | Mars | Oct. 23–Nov. 21 | A Scorpion can bring death with a sting, so this is the house of death. May die young. Very aggressive in a fight; will go to the end | Colon, bladder, gall bladder, sex organs |

IX	Sagittarius	the Archer	Jupiter	Nov. 22–Dec. 21	Characteristics of an arrow: swift, sudden, dashing. Implies boldness, freedom loving (as an arrow flies freely in the air . . .). Proud and refined (archers were elite troops in ancient times). "On target" with things like intuition.	Hips, thighs, sciatic nerve

(Leos are more fair, as lions are fairer in combat than scorpions). A two aspect sign: crafty, cunning like a scorpion, but this can turn toward helping men. Shift depends on other influences.

X	Capricorn	the Goat	Saturn	Dec. 22–Jan. 19	This is the winter solstice time. Days become longer. Time of rebirth. Combined with a goat's behavior, we can define Capricorns as noble, initiative (the "leaps" a goat makes), thrive on hardship and "leap over your adversaries in your climb to the heights."	Knee, joints, bones
XI	Aquarius	the Water Bearer	Saturn Uranus	Jan. 20–Feb. 18	Symbol is humanity progressing by giving aid to others (as the water bearers did). A "pouring forth" of great things. Refreshment and renewal. Aquarians therefore look to the future, believe in brotherhood, help mankind, and are generally first-class people.	Lower legs, ankles, blood circulation

XII Pisces the Fish Neptune Feb. 19– Two fish, plus watery clas- Feet
Mar. 20 sification makes this the
weakest sign. Sensitivity of
Pisceans can lead to dis-
solution or heights of imagination. Much discontent,
as a fish seems to have in
his aimless wanderings. Can
be very good in religion
and psychic aspects of life.

The basic qualities of each Sun sign, as one can see, derive from the mythology associated with the names rather arbitrarily given to the Zodiac by the ancients. If the Greeks used different names, or we happened to use an Arabic Zodiac, the eternal powers of each sign would be vastly different.

When the particular names of the Zodiac don't help, astrologers add the four elements:

Element	Signs	Characteristics
Fire	Aries, Leo, Sagittarius	Courage, leadership, forcefulness, action—people who are "on fire."
Earth	Taurus, Virgo, Capricorn	Practical, patient, concrete, generally "down-to-earth."
Air	Gemini, Libra, Aquarius	Intellectual and nervous, as in the expression "up in the air." Air carries sound, wind carries objects, so people in these signs can carry themselves to others, or communicate well. Good in speech ("windy"?).
Water	Cancer, Scorpio, Pisces	Generally "watery" and "weepy." Homeloving, tenderminded, affectionate. (Also, strong capacity for sex!)

Active signs include Cancer, Aries, Libra, and Capricorn. These people are active, creative, and conceive plans well.

Stable or fixed signs include Taurus, Leo, Scorpio, and Aquarius, whose sign bearers are positive and sustaining personalities.

The remaining signs—Gemini, Virgo, Sagittarius, and Pisces—are mutable or variable, which means they offer wisdom, philosophy, and insight behind the surface meaning of events.

Combine these basic qualities, which astrologers have amplified considerably over the years, and you have the general characteristics of the Sun sign for each person. The Sun sign is dominant, because of the historic importance attached to the sun. If this is all there were to astrology all of humanity would fit neatly into one of twelve personality types. This is so manifestly untrue that astrology needed to add more variables. Remember, the more variables, the more possible combinations . . . and the greater probability of hitting home with some part of the analysis of a certain human being.

The moon is one of the significant non-solar influences (Moon signs figure prominently in farmers' almanacs). In Evangeline Adams's words, the moon "shows the variety and quality just as the sun shows the type of and quality of the individuality. As the personality is the intimate and more immediate expression of the temperament and measures the quality and power of sense impression, and therefore the scope and precision of the mental forces, (the Moon) indirectly determines what we might call the fluid of being." The position of the moon in the signs is important, although less so by far than the solar position and, in the opinion of many astrologers, even less influential than the major planets.

Mercury and Venus hold special importance. They are closer to the sun and therefore more influential, a modern astrologer might explain. Actually, they move so fast that they are useful tools for differentiation because they add variables to the horoscopes of people born close together in time. The basic influences of these planets is as their mythological names suggest: Mercury, the winged messenger of God, active, fleet, tending to capriciousness as he moves from side to side of the sun; Venus, the daughter of Jove (Jupiter) is the personification of womanliness, life, art, rapture, receptivity, sensitivity, etc.

Mars, God of War, indicates fire, energy, strength. Jupiter is the chief God, father of Venus. He expresses expansion, material well-being, authority in a generally creative and enabling way. Saturn, the eldest of the Gods, reigned in a golden age of agriculture. The planetary influence is basically conservative; Saturn stabilizes in a more restrictive way than Jupiter. These planets move slowly and they are used for predicting long-term trends in one's life, more than defining specific characteristics of one's immediate personality. Uranus, Neptune, and Pluto, when incorporated into an astrological scheme, also have long-term tendencies. Generally, these "discovered" planets are considered to give indications of the future, openness to new things, and so forth.

Each sign has a ruling planet or planets. In addition, the signs may be subdivided into three descans of ten days each. The descans have ruling planets. Another scheme breaks signs into terms. In addition to this, each person has ruling planets for the day of his birth. The birth time influences him as well, through varying positions of the sun in its daily path about the skies.

All of this gives the astrologer enough descriptive material to cover just about any kind of human problem or personality. All the data for these variables comprise a very fat book. Much of the information is contradictory, at other times two aspects suggest compatible qualities. In any case, the astrologer's job is to sort through the grab bag of data to describe the client.

Miss Evangeline Adams, the queen of astrologers in the twenties and thirties (and who was the first to have her own radio broadcast until the National Association of Broadcasters prohibited such programs in their Code of Ethics), was arrested in 1914 in New York City for fortune-telling. She cast the judge's horoscope and he was so impressed by the mathematical, precise quality of the process he declared her not guilty. He added "Every fortune-teller is a violator of the law, but not every astrologer is a fortune-teller." Dr. Donald Kaplan, Greenwich Village psychoanalyst, told the *New York Times Magazine* that he felt part of the appeal of astrology lay in the way its systematized calculations parodied science. "It's a pop science. It has the same contempt, in a playful way, for science that pop art has for academic art."

When the horoscope chart is finished, the various elements are placed around a circle. Their geometric relationships reveal "aspects," which may be good or bad, depending on their angular relationship and which two planets are so related. Planets on the same radial line, or nearly the same, are in conjunction; separations of 30° (tendents), 60° (sextiles), and 120° (trigons) are, with conjunctions, generally favorable relationships; oppositions (180° relationships) and right angles (squares), unfavorable.

This is where the astrologer marshalls all his intuitive common sense and psychology. In a private horoscope session, my astrologer found herself dealing with a difficult subject. I am a Pisces. If one tells a Piscean the truth about himself, as one reading of the sign would have it, said Piscean would storm out disgusted and offended. Astrologically speaking, Pisces is the weakest sign and those who dwell in the Twelfth House reside in the loser's palace. We are given to mental instability, over-reaching ourselves, poor health, lack of control, and other debilitating character traits. No one is going to pay a fee to hear that he is a human reject.

As she unfolded my psyche bit by bit, she looked up from my horoscope in a manner that suggested she was reading my own responses as closely as her chart. I don't wear a good poker face, so I probably gave her ample nonverbal clues. Anyway, she worked through my descan (the third descan ruled by Mars, which is better than the others) and noted I was born on the cusp (near the end or beginning of a sign) which leaves room for influences of the next sign. The net result was a profile that emphasized the stronger sides of a Pisces. For example, my characteristic sensitivity seemed to lead toward creativity and religious interest, rather than dissolution.

I had read in one book or another just about everything she had to say, although she was unaware of my research. Her unique ability to weave all the possibilities for a Piscean—and they are nearly infinite, as with any sign—into a pretty accurate profile of myself, as I see me at least, was quite remarkable. I would judge better than half of her comments were valid. Her advice—"Watch money matters with great care" and "Be careful of snap judgments that can hurt your career"—seemed less appropriate. I am basically rather close with a dollar and generally not impulsive with personal judgments. However, it is as hard to knock such advice as it is to declare motherhood a sin. I paid my money and left. I suspect anyone seeing this particular woman would get his money's worth, if he used an ounce or two of common sense.

Two psychology professors from Northwestern University, James Bryan and Lee Sechrest, sent identical letters a couple of years ago to eighteen astrologers who advertised in astrological magazines offering counseling services. Each letter described the same marital difficulty. They finally concluded, in their report published in the respected scholarly journal *Transaction,* that the advice they got back was not only undamaging, but actually a bargain. Their criteria for useful advice—being adequate to the situation, inexpensive, prompt, practical, credible, and friendly— were met by the astrologers they consulted. They, of course, disclaimed any support for the premises of the art, but they thought the interpretations of the horoscopes relating to their hypothetical problem were loose enough for anyone with good sense to gain some meaningful benefit.

This general looseness of expression and one's ability to read himself into the stated horoscope is astrology's great survival point. Actually, each sign of the Zodiac contains characteristics of all persons. Reading one is like reading a book on abnormal psychology. Everyone has some paranoid or schizophrenic components in his personality. Students of psychology, along with their colleagues in medical schools, often read themselves so completely into their texts that they imagine themselves the victims of every pathology. The chances of some aspect of your horoscope ringing true are very high, but a similar probability holds for any other sign as well, besides your own. Better than chance readings depend on a skillful astrologer whose subjective interpretation of the astral data is related to à grasp of practical psychology, or else on one's willingness or sheer desire to believe the horoscope is right. In either case, the loose and general language astrologers use saves the day.

Generalized language makes collective horoscopes possible. Collective horoscopes are the ones you read in your newspaper, or purchase in horoscope magazines and books. They apply to all the designated people, and are not personal. On a given day about three years ago, Jeane Dixon told her syndicated column readers that Aries people would enjoy "Another in a series of unpressured Sundays. Take full advantage. Join forces with friends at church and gatherings."[4] Carroll Righter told his Aries readers that day:

4. December 15, 1968. © Newsday.

"A good day to reach true understanding with associates so that the future will be much more successful. The right sort of amusements with mate, or other congenials is fine now. Be generous."[5] Both agree on being with friends, which is logical for these are Sunday horoscope suggestions and Sunday is usually a congenial day with friends. The other advice has a general agreement, but in any case one must admit it is good advice and certainly not harmful. On the same day, Miss Dixon told Taurus people to "Expect crankiness from loved ones in the early evening" while Mr. Righter told the same group they were able to ". . . accomplish a very great deal now. . . . Take that finery out and make a big impression on others."

These two suggestions seem more at variance than those for Aries folks, but such collective horoscopes are like headlines in the newspaper: they only skim the surface. Many astrologers view them as bunk, or as "a necessary evil to make a living." Contradictions in these capsule astrological summaries can't make a case against the art.

But when Miss Dixon tells her readers to expect crankiness from loved ones, she is treading on potentially dangerous ground. Miss Dixon is personally a very sensitive and spiritual woman, more given to psychic and intuitive predictions than to classic astrology. Yet, telling people to expect something is liable to create the condition itself. If we believe something will happen to us, it actually might because we subconsciously wish it to happen. A person expecting to fight with his wife on Sunday evening may well spend the afternoon shooting out the clues to his mate that he is gunning for female bear. By nightfall, the fireworks start . . . and the horoscope comes true.

On the other hand, properly understood, this could be helpful advice. If you read it as words to prepare you for a possibility, you might take extra care to be patient and pleasant with your loved ones Sunday evening. In that case—whether the whole bit is true or false—it accomplishes some social good.

In *Pisces: Your Day-by-Day Zodiac International 1971 Horo-*

5. December 15, 1968. Reprinted through the courtesy of McNaught Syndicate, Inc.

scope and Character Analysis,[6] Simon and Schuster's entry into the booming horoscope handbook market, the authors take pains to make it clear that negative items in a day's forecast shouldn't discourage you. "Do not assume that days marked difficult are entirely unfortunate, but use the descriptions as a guide, in a general way, as to what to avoid.

"And, when 'difficult' days are mentioned, they are not always adverse for all activities; but special care must be used. . . ."

This same handbook cites April 6, 1971 as a "disturbing" day for Pisceans. It explains that "Marital or partnership affairs are likely to be difficult, with arguments possible. You can help matters by being more willing to cooperate. Business affairs will probably be interfered with. Your personal plans are likely to meet opposition." April 8 is "disquieting." It says this is "Not an active day but continued tact with close associates will be necessary." Notice how each "beware" has an accompanying "corrective." On days when difficulties may crop up, a little tact and willingness to cooperate will smooth over the bumps. Tact and cooperation are generally good virtues; surely anyone who follows them on April 6 and 8 of 1971 will improve their chances for a good day.

Astrology, in its modern dress, definitely strives to become a life-expanding and liberating force. This sounds strange to some whose minds are filled with the stellar terrors of ancient times, such as Lucretius fought against. But everything grows up and changes, and not the least of the maturing philosophies is the occult. One astrologer told me, "The stars are given by God to guide us. They are signposts for our lives, clues about our destiny. They do not control us or determine our actions. We are free people. But why ignore this gift of God? It is knowledge that can help us tremendously. If we know some general trends in our character, and we have a picture of some possibilities before us, we are well armed. We can meet life with our inner resources and conquer all the things that paralyze life. Astrology is a means

---

6. *Pisces: Your Day-by-Day Zodiac International 1971 Horoscope and Character Analysis,* © 1970 by Simon & Schuster, Inc. Reprinted by permission of Essandess Special Editions/division of Simon and Schuster, Inc.

toward true human development, real maturity of each unique individual."

Not every follower of astrology has caught the message of liberation. A business executive told me a story about his secretary. Fundamentally an outgoing and alive kind of person, on certain days she would withdraw from people, become quiet, passive, very careful in her relationships with others. He mused about this for a long time. Her moods didn't seem to folow the hormonal cycles of womanhood, and he was at a loss to figure her out. One day, he discovered she was dedicated to astrology. He talked with her about her interest in the stars and this solved his mystery. On those days when she withdrew, her horoscope pointed to troubles and she wanted to play it cool. She obviously let astrology run her life instead of guiding it creatively. Those who refuse to date Leos because they are "incompatible" and people who reject others right away because their sign doesn't fit well are slicing themselves off from a lot of human joy. Treated in this way, astrology can be limiting and conducive to prejudice.

But it need not completely hamper human growth. Astrological morality is very much "do your own thing, be free, conquer and make good." The stars never tell you to "take up your cross" or to give your life for someone else. That is why astrology is so much in keeping with the modern mood of self-fulfillment. It is, probably, a basically selfish outlook, which is one historic reason why classic Christianity has opposed astrology.

However, the word selfish, in our day, has taken on new meaning. Jesus' dictum, "Love your neighbor as yourself" has shifted its accent to "yourself." We know from psychological studies that the person who cannot love himself, cannot love others; the man who cannot find himself, cannot find others.

Astrology does help people find themselves. In a time when we have a banquet of possible life-styles before us, when we are urged to be ourselves and "personal integrity" is the moral watchword that "moderation" or "restraint" used to be, the seeker after self-identity is searching for some kind of guidance. Astrology helps them sort out life-styles. It is a form of typology, similar to Sheldon's famous endomorphs, ectomorphs, and mesomorphs, which catalogued human personalities by the shape of their bodies. Schemes to classify the incomprehensible variety of human personalities fill a definite need. They give us some much needed take-hold points. The problem is, we take these schemes as gospel; they are beguilingly simple and human nature continues proudly to defy simplistic categories.

A young woman who enthusiastically followed astrology told me she never read her horoscope in advance of the day. Instead, she examined the data each evening, as a way of reflecting on the day's events. "If you know what is going to happen before it happens, it takes all the fun out of life. I enjoy surprises, but I am also deeply interested in knowing myself. I am an Aquarian; I am convinced that this Sun sign and I are made for each other. It is perfect. Each night I go over what happened to me and compare it with various readings about that day for an Aquarian. This helps me sort things out and find their meaning. Personally, I just don't dig this predictive stuff, but I think astrology is a tremendous help in understanding what has already happened to you."

This is one approach to astrological self-understanding. Scientific and psychologically inclined people may dismiss it as bunk, but the organization of one's self into some kind of whole personality involves working with myths and symbols. It is much more religious an exercise than it is a psychological one. Psychoanalysis, for instance, deals with personality integration and it is filled with myths, abstract constructs, and relatively unsupported constructs. But in working with people, this mix affords more therapy than the tightly controlled, almost mechanical work of behaviorist psychologists, whose biggest success seems to be with rats. Of all the available myths, astrology is less harmful than some, if it is properly understood and used with a dash of common sense.

In any case, the people who count on astrology for a peek into the future will be disappointed. Modern astrology only claims that the stars show trends, but do not determine actual behavior, which is up to each person's free will. A fatalistic personality may find aspects of astrology that comfort his desire to be controlled, but the distortion is in the eye of the believer, not in astrology. Some people even have given Christianity a powerfully fatalistic twist because of their own need to feel this way.

Another girl told me that she had found a sense of oneness with the cosmos through astrology. This girl has been raised in the Christian tradition, but had never really felt part of the whole universe. "In astrology, I find my place in the whole big picture," she told me. "It makes me feel important; not just one little creature, you know, but, well, part of the whole big universe." This girl was far on the path toward a mystical faith, which is where the occult often leads its serious followers.

Not everyone is this serious, of course. Religious and philosophical reflection seems to be a rare gift, distributed with great economy by whoever controls man's abilities. A good many astrology buffs, perhaps the vast majority, find it a kicky thing to do, something that is "in" and makes for fresh conversation over cocktails. These people play with the art: "I don't know. Maybe there is something to it. Anyway, it is fun, sometimes helpful, and it isn't going to hurt me." Or, they find some kind of identity and differentiation from the masses of faces that fill this world by taking their Sun sign as another name. "I am an Aquarian!" becomes a slogan of pride; it makes one feel good, as the knowledge that your great-grandfather was a famous general might have accomplished in another era.

Among younger people, astrology becomes a dating game. Instead of "Haven't I seen you before?", the new world male opens with, "Say, I bet you're a Sagittarius!" Translated, that means, "When I looked at you I thought you were refined, poised, healthy, sports-minded and you like to be admired." Some people guess very well, and tossing out the more favorable Sun signs can be a form of compliment. And if the signs of the budding lovers are compatible—such as a Pisces and a Capricorn—it is another clue that "We are made for each other."

Traditional Christian churches have not thought much of astrology in the last couple of centuries, no matter what kind of case can be made for the art. The church objects on four grounds, which hasn't slowed down the growth of astrology very much, especially among church oriented young people who seem as keen on astrology as their non-churchgoing friends.

First, the church is actually very rationalistic in its way of thinking. Its theology may be grounded in events such as Jesus' Resurrection, whose significance is a matter of pure faith, but the apparatus built upon these faith premises is quite logical. Since the days when the church fought Darwin's evolution and lost all the battles except on the Tennessee front, theologians have accommodated the scientific world view into the Christian faith as much as possible. Modern biblical scholars emphasize that their work is "scientific," by which they mean they treat the sacred texts in the same critical manner as any other ancient document. This is a far cry from the devotional, pious approach toward the Bible which revered each word as holy in itself. As a result, church thinkers find themselves rejecting astrology for the same reasons scientists do: it is unprovable, it is a hoax, it is a complex house built on intellectual swamps. The same comment can be made about theology, of course, but devoted believers in one mythical-religious system (be it Christianity or Marxism) will accept their own shaky premises, their personal elements of pure faith, while casting a critical eye on anyone else who tries the same thing. Astrology can rightly be termed a competitor to the Christian faith, which is a source of much of the church's opposition. But this is a far cry form asying it is either wrong or fundamentally opposed to Christian theology.

The second objection stems from a sounder theological basis. God, in the Judeo-Christian tradition, is the primary actor on the stage of the world. All things come from him, even faith and grace. His will is supreme. One's destiny is in God, the one and holy God of Scriptures. Stars, moon phases, planets—anything but God himself is a false symbol, a wrong sign, a delusion, an idol. Monotheistic faiths often develop systems of intermediaries, such as angels in the Christian tradition, but these always tend to dilute the uniqueness and oneness of God Himself. The early church wrestled for years trying to find a way to reconcile Jesus, the Father, and the Holy Spirit, before they settled on the strange phrasing of the Trinitarian doctrine. What was at stake, of course, was the notion of one supreme God.

Astrology grew up in polytheistic environments such as Babylonia and Greece. The montheistic Old Testament writers, especially, rejected it vehemently, on the grounds that it was damned by its association with worshipers of many gods. Modern astrologers with a religious bent try to accommodate their art to Christianity by asserting that God has given the stars, sun, and planets as signs and guides for us. They are, in a sense, messengers (angels) of God. The church has never sanctioned or officially blessed any channels for God's dealings with men other than the classic media of the Word and the Sacraments. However, the idea of asking God for a "sign," by way of indicating his answer to prayer, is a common practice among conservative evangelical believers. This is somewhat different, obviously, from astrological signs, but it indicates that even devout Christians look for tangible guidance from their spiritual Father.

The third objection comes from those Christian groups who maintain a conviction that the Devil is alive and well. Most Christians allow the loving God to flow over them and envelope them in goodness and grace. They don't like the idea of a powerful and personified force of evil in the world. Early Christians spoke a great deal about the Evil One, but many modern Christians abandoned the doctrine of a personal Satan because they became enmeshed in the basically secular view of man's innate goodness and unlimited potential for progress. The believers who still share St. John's view of Christ wrestling the Devil for control of the world simply add astrology to the long list of the Devil's works which believers must meet head on before Satan leads another soul into spiritual bondage. This point of view has some merit, because the occult can lead people into slavery of fear and the despair of uncontrollable forces. A few Christians over the years, one must add in all fairness, have also succumbed to fear and terror within the framework of the Christian faith.

A fourth objection to astrology, from the viewpoint of traditional Christianity, is that the astral art supports a selfish morality. The notion of man corralling the powers of the heavens in order to became Master of his Destiny strikes the classic faith as monumental egocentricity. Man is a creature of God and this overweening pride is his downfall, as the story of Adam, in a common interpretation, made plain. The fall of Lucifer, more a traditional legend than a scriptural certainty, is another example of creatures trying to be like God. Pride is a Christian sin, often talked about as the essence of sin itself. Furthermore, a morality that stresses self-fulfillment and personal advantage will not adjust comfortably to the historic Christian posture of sacrificial living. The obvious fact is that the church has itself failed to live up to its own principles.

Only a handful of avant-garde theologians, such as Harvey Cox, perceive any way in which astrology can come into the Christian home as a permanent guest. These thinkers look on religion, and Christianity, as a mental trip, a way to transcend oneself and enlarge self-awareness. Such men also appreciate the religious value of play and of fun. They are willing to consider anything that helps someone accomplish this kind of spiritual voyage. Astrology doesn't happen to be the best occult art for such a trip, but many do make it on the tails of the stars. Generally, it is safe to say that astrology won't be baptized into the faith in the foreseeable future. The church will still oppose it. How violent this opposition becomes depends on how tolerant a pastor or theologian feels toward people who play around with non-Christian symbol systems.

At the same time, the fact that astrology spreads like an epidemic in our day, even within committed Christian circles, must tell the church something. If astrology as such can be dismissed with a smile, the dynamic that drives people to its comforting breast cannot be so lightly tossed out. It expresses some deeply felt needs of many people: the need for self-identity, the need for guidance in day-to-day living, the need to be free enough to discover the new "selfishness," the need to feel they are important, and the need to sense they belong to the mystifying universe. To this long list can be added one more: the need to find security in an insanely changing world.

For centuries, the church has claimed to have a system that satisfies these needs, but the growth of astrology indicates that the traditional symbols used by the church to communicate its message no longer get through to people. They start looking elsewhere. Astrology may be a message from God after all, a word of judgment to his church that they aren't making the good news of the faith sparkling enough to help people where they need help. ☿

3

Previews of Coming

Attractions

Astrology's credentials as a method of predicting the specific future events withered after centuries of bad records.[1] So, astrology turned toward generalized character analysis and vague admonitions about the worth of certain days. If you seek more concrete, specific peeks into tomorrow and beyond, you still have hope. The best professional astrologers may not give you assurance that the stars determine tomorrow with precision, but a host of other divination techniques offer some method of getting a hold on the future.

Prophecy, in this concrete sense, has a long history. A large number of prophets have been and are intuitive psychics. We can discuss them later. For the moment, let us examine some common nonintuitive techniques of prognostication.

Criswell, an old man with bleached blond hair and Liberace-style garments, works the prophet game out of Los Angeles. He has become a favorite guest on the *Tonight* show when it does a stand in Hollywood. Criswell's prophetic abilities have blessed our world for a long time. I remember watching his show on Los Angeles TV when I was in high school. Criswell is one kind of

1. Most recently, California failed to slip into the Pacific in 1969 as predicted by some astrologers.

future diviner: he reads a lot of newspapers and "insider" news-letters such as *Kiplinger Reports.* They may, for example, mention a drought somewhere in India; Criswell then predicts that "thousands and thousands will soon die in Asia and there will be terrible plagues of disease." He prophesies the future by projecting some reasonable consequences from present occurrences. A drought in India usually leads to famine which leads to massive starvation which means many unburied bodies and that can cause epidemics. He pushes a bit of information to its furthest conclusion and announces his prediction.

Criswell is a showman extraordinary, but his game is the same one we all play. His favorite line, "We are all interested in the future, for the future is where we will spend the rest of our lives" is only too true. All of us want to know about tomorrow and the next day.

That is why we willingly accept statistical predictions, which point to future events on the basis of past performance—because we believe in science deep inside our bones. It is also a fairly reliable method.

But what if a friend said, "Well, I killed a pigeon this morning and spilled its entrails on the ground. From the way the intestines curled in a spiral form, I knew that a depression was on its way." At this point, we have gone into the world of occult divination. Occult divination derives the future from things that have no apparent causal relationship to the forthcoming event.

Prediction in the short term is a dangerous game. People will remember the prophecy when the time for fulfillment comes. And it had better be right. None of the scientific techniques for prediction work in the very short term. They cannot, for instance, accurately predict *tomorrow's* Dow Jones stock average. Over a period of a year or so, however, they can give reliable clues about general trends, if all variable factors hold constant. The unforeseen event, such as a war or sudden change in public mood, hampers the modern prognosticator as devilishly as it did his ancestral colleagues.

The general feeling of resentment toward Big Brother scientific predictive techniques opens the ordinary man to more "human" forms of divining the future—methods in which the individual figures prominently. This fast-growing mood of hostility toward highly organized scientific methods creates the climate in which occult divination can flourish.

How else can one explain the fact that Ouija boards sell almost as fast as Monopoly games? A Ouija board uses a marker which can move across a board and point toward words that suggest answers. The user places his hand on the marker and concentrates on the question. Almost imperceptible muscular movements cause the marker to slide over the smooth board until it comes to rest. The feat requires concentration because these motions (similar to those in automatic writing) result from a low-grade, self-induced trance, close to hypnosis in character. A Ouija board "works"; in fact, it represents an objective picture of subconscious mental activity. Fascinating as this is psychologically, it doesn't have much to do with prediction, except in so far as a good Ouija operator comes up with answers that he already holds in his subconscious, because our inner wishes often guide our actions and tend to fulfill themselves.

Historically, divination was the queen of the occult arts, because ruler and peasant alike desperately wanted to know the path that lay before them. "Forewarned is forearmed" is a slogan with much truth. The modern businessman rephrases it as "Information is power," i.e., the more you know about tomorrow's possibilities, the more successful you become. However, beginning sometime in the middle or late middle nineteenth century, divination slid down the hierarchy of occult practice to the basement of the art. This time roughly coincides with the beginnings of reliable statistical analysis. One would guess this is a classic example of how science triumphs over superstition and crushes beneath its rational heel. But that is not quite true. Divination is still with us in many forms, and some of them have a touch of pseudoscience to improve their standings.

Palmistry, crystal gazing, card reading, tea leaf analysis—the forms of fortune-telling we know today—were the poor handmaidens of divination in the past. Their predominance in modern divination suggests how low this once great speciality has slipped.

The ancients relied heavily on animal entrails to indicate the future. A layman often assumes that the way an animal's intestine coils won't vary from creature to creature. This little fiction gets reinforced by our biology books, which always show one stylized and representative diagram of the internal organs of an animal. For example, we think all human stomachs are identical, just like the neat wine-bag shape we see in a biology text. Doctors know much better; Anson's *Atlas of Human Anatomy* shows at least twelve vastly different, though "normal," human stomach shapes. Other animals enjoy the same variety in their organs.

Such a situation is ideal for divination. Divination techniques need some way to set up variables—either arranging cards in some random sequence, or using a given variable, such as the lines on the palm of a hand or the ways an intestine curls. The more variables in a given system, the greater the possible combinations of significance, and therefore the greater chance of being right. Also, the more complicated the scheme of interpretation becomes, the more arcane and mysterious it looks to the layman. Possession of such mysterious knowledge is essential for the diviner who wishes to become a professional; if anyone can do it, he is soon out of a job.

Mesopotamia, the wellspring of Western civilization, provided the ground on which divination entered our lives. A favorite Babylonian technique is called hepatoscopy—divination by reading animal livers. We have about 700 tablets which contain prophecies obtained through looking at the liver. Why the Babylonians selected the liver—as many primitive people do even today—is still a mystery. We do know that the ancients conceived of the liver as the seat of life and existence, much in the same way we now speak of the heart or the brain. Livers are also easy to identify and remove.

Hepatoscopy became a solemn act of state for Babylonian kings. They thought so much of this procedure that its use was limited to work on behalf of kings and nobility. A seer would remove the liver from an animal and take it to the altar of the god who controlled his client's future. There he would examine the condition of this organ; checking its shape, the number and position of the convolutions, the arrangement of the blood vessels, in order to determine dates and results of such state activities as war and palace overthrows. The seer would submit a written report on his findings—some of which archaeologists have discovered—to his client. These seers were highly respected and held positions of honor, so long as they were right. A bad error usually cost the prophet his life.

We have no way of telling how many seers, under extreme pressures of life and death to accomplish a successful prophecy, departed from the rules of liver reading and used their own common sense and understanding of the political situation to frame their final report. The rules for hepatoscopy have come down to us on clay tablets which seers used to teach pupils their art. Like many mysterious things, hepatoscopy eventually became routinized and finally dryly formulated in textbooks. Some of these tablets for teaching date back to 2000 B.C. and have been found at such famous digs as Hattus, Megiddo (in Palestine) and Tell Hariri.

The Babylonian peasant, forbidden the luxuries of hepatoscopy and other divination methods controlled by the nobility, settled for folk divination, based on omens and proverbs. They knew, for instance, that a snake found coiled in a man's bed portended that his wife would roll up her eyes and sell her children. Birds, and how they flew, comprised a large part of this folk wisdom. Abnormalities, even the birth of twins, were generally deemed bad omens.

This separation of divination technology along class lines might explain the origin of our folk wisdom about omens and portents. The common man in Western countries draws from the dark wells of hand-me-down omens. The Italian farmer knows all about the Evil Eye and how to combat its terrible influence; sophisticated New York executives go out of their way to avoid passing under a ladder or allowing a black cat to cross their path. Spilling salt is another popular omen of bad fortune, unless one takes corrective measures. (This particular omen is related to the great value placed on salt in the olden times; a scarce commodity, it was nevertheless essential to life and spilling it wastefully could be a costly mistake.) A host of folk omens connected with childbearing survive into the modern era: women who are frightened while with child give birth to deformities; a mother who views a cripple or dwarf will bear a misshapen child; and many other tales even a modern obstetrician must work to dispel.

The Romans used state diviners or *haruspices* on a full-time basis. The Romans, for all their sound administration and superb legal minds, sopped up divination like a sponge. The *haruspices* exerted tremendous power over the affairs of state, becoming perhaps the most powerful group of occultists in history. They looked for guidance from the gods in thunder, lightning, behavior of birds and beasts, and by the entrails of birds and animals. These magicians had the power, under the Republic, to suspend all business whenever bad omens suggested that such a measure seemed wise. Again, we cannot tell how seriously they followed the wisdom of their profession, or how open they were to more common-sensical and politically expedient interpretations. Their professionalism is questioned by their tendency to find bad omens and close off governmental business whenever a measure unpopular with the aristocratic Senate came before the popular Assembly.

In medieval Europe, divination arts captured the imagination of all classes of men and women. Magic in those days was more one piece of cloth than the remnant effect given by the chapters in this book would indicate. Alchemy, the Cabala, some witchcraft, trances, divination, and astrology could easily be practiced by one person, called the magus, or magician. Methods for predicting the future grew phenomenally, as did the collection of good and evil portents. The intermingling of traditions within this rich occult heritage stopped and specialization set in toward more modern times. Today, the occultist tends to be a specialist in one of the branches of the art. Relatively few are comprehensive "magicians" in the medieval sense, although a recovery of a sense of oneness about magic is beginning to make an impact in occult circles.

Crystal ball gazing, also known as crystomancy or scrying, now has become a form of show business suited to gypsy types who neither dance nor sing well. We enjoy it purely as entertainment, which is quite a comedown from its past glories. The original crystal ball gazers took their art seriously and managed their divinations in a trance state. The modern practitioner has probably never entered a trance; she settles for telling you Mr. Tall-Dark-Handsome-Moneybags is peeking around the corner of your future.

The glass ball originally served to concentrate the attention of the magician. Any shiny material would do, if a glass ball wasn't available. This enabled the seer to enter into a trance, by a process we would call self-hypnosis. Medieval gazers began with prayer and the drawing of pentagrams or five-pointed stars (which are prominent magical symbols). They would burn candles and recite incantations. All of this apparatus helped induce a trance state. If the magician couldn't make it to the next mental level, he would employ a teen-ager. Adolescents are more open to suggestion and trances, while tending toward eidetic imagery (ability to recall detailed pictures of what one has seen before). Whatever visions came in the trance, or whatever words the magician uttered while off on his trip, constituted the prophecy. It gained its credibility from its uniqueness: most advice comes from ordinary people in conscious states, and so the words of one in a mysterious trance must come from those with whom he communes in his transcendental sphere. Maybe even God himself. Or some chief power of darkness.

Palmistry has also come on bad times in our day. It is a fun game, described in cheap manuals. Few palm readers bother with a trance state, although they may indulge in a little hocus-pocus. Most of them simply examine your palm, looking at its major lines, and interpreting the subtle variations. Quite often, they achieve remarkable results. I had my palm read by a no-nonsense type, who dispensed with the mystery and got right down to the analysis. We were strangers, yet she determined my career, revealed my family size, and told me things about my life and habits which she could not have known through other means. One cannot test how much my palm lines played in her analysis. She was a sensitive young woman, probably prone to the psychic, and such people often have an intuitive grasp of human nature. I tried palm reading using a book for guidance, but I had far less success. It

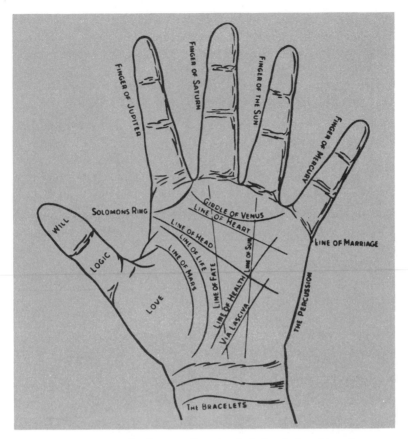

For most people they are lines in their hand, but for palmistry they are a gold mine of information about your future.

seems that in this area of the occult, as in any other, the human element plays a large part in the final outcome. The key to the process lies in interpreting the variations in lines, and all of this skill cannot be put into manuals.

Cards are another popular form of divining the future and have been used that way for centuries. Playing cards came to Europe about the fourteenth century. Besides the cards with which we are familiar, the pip and court cards, these early decks added some others for a total of seventy-eight cards. An extra twenty-two cards, now lost from our decks, were called tarots or *triomphes*

51

(trumps), because they had a higher value when played in combination with the ordinary or numeral cards.

The Tarot cards feature dramatic, graphic illustrations.

These twenty-two cards won't be found in your bridge deck, but you can purchase them. Ask for Tarot Cards. In the fourteenth to sixteenth centuries, these particular cards took on magic significance. They are emblematic cards, with pictures of a Magician, High Priestess (female Pope), Empress, Emperor, Falling Tower, Wheel of Fortune, Justice, and other things along with some grim scenes of Last Judgment, Devil, and Hanged Man. Eliphas Levi, who compiled a lot of ancient magical lore about a century ago, compiled a table of significance for the Tarot trumps. The Magician stands for being, spirit, man, primitive life force. The Devil represented occult science, mystery, magic, and moral strength—an interesting combination of attributes! The Last Judgment stood for eternal life and the generative powers of the earth. The Empress symbolized the triad, or group of three, relationships in all their forms. By laying out the cards and interpreting their sequence according to what they symbolized, the magician or seer would predict what lay ahead for his client. Tarot reading is more sophisticated than palm reading, because the cards have mystical associations. Some have straightforward meanings, such as good, weakness, and so forth. But the cards which indicate forces such as the generative powers of earth, outpouring of thought, or Being, open the way for a mystical interpretation of Destiny and Life that goes beyond discovering whether or not you are going to win a certain promotion.

The association of magic and mysticism is characteristic of cabalistic practices. This form of Jewish mysticism grew up during the Middle Ages and has exerted tremendous influence on the course of magic and the occult in the Western world, both in Christian and non-Christian circles. It is strange and mysterious indeed, but its fascination seems eternal. A number of "higher wisdom" cults today (such as the Rosicrucians or AMORC) still draw heavily upon cabalistic writers.

The Tarot trumps probably gained their special status through a coincidence. There are twenty-two Tarots, and there are twenty-two letters in the Hebrew alphabet. The Hebrew letters were held in high esteem by both Jewish and Christian occultists, and Hebrew words appear in magical incantations from every European country. This may be due to the overwhelming influence of the Cabala on magic, and to the Jewish background of the cabalistic writers. However, Christian occultists were open to the appeal of Hebrew because it was a holy tongue, a scriptural language—the one in which God's proper name (YHWH or Yahweh) must not be spoken.

Hebrew, as Latin and some other languages, uses letters to indicate numbers. (Our present numerical symbols come to us from the Arabs.) Most magic and divination relies on words, but when the components of words—letters—also have a number meaning, it is but a short step to numerology, or the art of predicting the future through numbers.

Because all letters in the Hebrew alphabet have numerical meanings, this language is particularly well suited to numerology. Medieval magicians formed magic words in Hebrew by constructing a magic number and converting it to a word. Each Tarot card was assigned a Hebrew letter and corresponding numerical number, all of which added to the cards' magical meaning.

Each number has a significance, especially the first twelve. Twelve seems a favorite number, perhaps deriving from the twelve houses of the Zodiac. One represents unity—God, creative purpose, even the hierarchy of objects that epitomize parts of life, such as the soul and heart. Number one also can represent Lucifer. Two is the number of light, friendship, courage, marriage, clarity. Three is a number of totality, because it is a triad and has associations with the Trinity and such verbal triads as "past, present, and future." Five is the number of justice, because it balances in the middle of the first ten numbers. Ten is a number of completion, representing the whole life. Twelve is the number of perfection and grace, because Christ plus eleven faithful apostles make twelve.

We all experience the powers of numbers. Who hasn't had qualms about number thirteen? Many Americans thought the ill-fated Apollo 13 mission to the moon was doomed from the start because of its unlucky number. Some hotels, apartment, and office buildings discreetly skip the thirteenth floor, and jump from the twelfth to the fourteenth. Most of us cherish a "special" number. Favorite numbers vary with civilizations. The Amerindians liked four, while the Chinese chose five. Babylonians selected seven as their favorite, and this has come into our culture as Lucky Seven.

We live in a world of new style numerology. At least, we have come to respect numbers beyond all reason. Anything we can quantify and deal with mathematically seems more certain than information we must use verbally. Science has taught us a new power of numbers, and it is an open question whether we now merely respect numbers, quantities and numerical operations, or whether we frankly worship them.

Numerology is associated with mathematics in the same way that astrology and astronomy have historic connections. In the beginnings of science, thinkers confused rational thought and magic. Our science textbooks politely overlook the arcane side of their founders, so we recognize Tycho Brahe as a pioneer in astronomy, without knowing that he also followed astrology. In math, Pythagoras of Samos, about sixth century B.C., is a similar case. Every high-school student knows of the Pythagorean Theorem, by which the hypotenuse of a right triangle can be found through the length of its two sides. Besides being a genius at math, he wallowed in mysticism and the occult. We owe to him the basic system for giving "meanings" to numbers. He called four the number of justice, and we still speak of a "square deal." Ten was his perfect number, because it was made by adding a sequence of one plus two plus three plus four. He founded a mystical school of philosophy, which influenced Plato and later philosophers. His followers adopted as their emblem ten dots arranged in an inverted triangle:

```
*  *  *  *
 *  *  *
  *  *
   *
```

We also owe to Pythagoras the mystical meaning of the pentagram or five-pointed star, which is still being used as a magical symbol.

Pythagoras dealt with rational numbers—numbers which can be expressed exactly in a combination of integers. There are also irrational numbers. For example, the number we call *pi,* which can never be completely expressed even if one extended 3.1415-926536 . . . on to infinity. Pythagoreans discovered these irrational numbers, but kept the news to themselves because it would blow numerology, as they knew it, to pieces. The secret finally leaked out about 410 B.C., but the Pythagorean fears were unfounded. Irrational numbers did not destroy the holding power of numerology on the human mind.

Dreams offer us all a free form of entertainment. The strangeness of a dream, in which everything seems at once real and unreal, bringing us joy, dread, or even sexual climax, fascinates the modern man, even with his scientific resources. Psychiatrists probe their meaning, psychologists try to find the mechanism or cause of dreams, but they still remain shrouded in intellectual fog. Small wonder then that people accept dreams as interventions in their lives that have powerful meanings, if properly understood.

Sigmund Freud and his pupils gave a lot of attention to dreams. Freud felt that they represented hidden wishes and desires. Through dreams, he felt he could probe the unconscious mind of his patient. Because Freudian theory concentrates on the Eros or sexual force in man, his dream interpretations take on sexual connotations. The problem for a psychoanalyst is interpreting a dream. If a woman reports a series of dreams over a long period in which she was in a well or a cave and a long pole, or powerful masculine symbol such as a lion, came toward her, a psychiatrist may safely interpret this as a repressed wish for intercourse, or perhaps a fear of sexual relationships, depending on whether she spoke of dreams or nightmares. Phallic symbolism such as this may reveal hidden sexual desires and the doctor may accept them as such if other evidence indicates that this interpretation is valid. Psychiatric dream interpretation is a cautious business, requiring the analyst to weigh several factors and use sound professional judgment.

Interpretive dream books, written by nonpsychiatrically trained authors, sell on newsstands to a vast audience. These little manuals clearly explain the significance of every element in a dream. One cannot use them simply, however. First, a dream may have many elements which have contradictory meanings and the user has to evaluate which one predominates. Usually, he will select the most congenial meaning. Second, different dream books give various readings of the same symbol. In one, a fast automobile ride may suggest that a journey is in the dreamer's future, while another manual will tell the seeker that this means danger ahead.

Numerology lends a hand to dream interpretation. If the particular symbol is confusing, perhaps the ways in which the symbols group have meanings. The key to a dream about receiving ten ten-dollar bills may not be in the symbol of money, but in the prominent role of the number ten. Because the content of our dreams are so variable and open to such flexible interpretation, they are natural sources for occult prediction.

The Greeks laid great stress on predicting the future through dreams (called oneiromancy). The noted Greek historian Herodotus, in the fifth century B.C., tells us that when King Xerxes of Persia contemplated his invasion of Greece, his uncle Artaban tried to talk him out of it. But in a series of dreams, a godlike figure came to Xerxes and urged him to go ahead with his invasion plans. Xerxes then asked his uncle to sleep in the royal couch and, behold, Uncle Artaban had the same dream. With such impressive information, Xerxes launched his invasion right away. It was, as you know, a total disaster.

Everyone has heard stories, or had actual experiences, of premonitory dreams that really did come to pass. A man told me he dreamed his wife was leaving him for another man. It was a terrifying dream, because he assumed that his marriage was reasonably tranquil. He remembered his shock and pain when his wife, in the dream, announced her intention to leave him. About five weeks later, his wife confronted him with just that demand— in the living room, where she had talked to him in his dream.

"Later," he went on, "I met the man who was her lover. In my dream, this man met her at the door as she left our house and I saw him clearly. When I met him, my recollection of the dream flooded my mind. It was astounding, but he looked just like he did in that dream, yet he was a man I personally had never met before."

There are several possible explanations for this phenomenon. He may have had unconscious guilt about his marriage, telling himself all was well when he knew at a deeper level that he was ignoring his wife terribly, because of his preoccupation with business. Our memory of a dream is very selective; we do not recall all that went on and awaken with only the highlights fixed in our consciousness. Therefore, we can easily read events into a dream which weren't there. When this man recognized his wife's lover, it could be that he read back into his dream features and appearances which weren't there originally. He had already been troubled by the strange fulfillment of the dream and could well be predisposed to find additional points where reality and the dream coincided. This kind of explanation, though, doesn't persuade the person who, for one reason or the other, wishes to believe in the effective predictive powers of dreams.

There is a sense in which dreams do have a possibility of coming to pass. The psychiatrist C. G. Jung speaks of "prospective" dreams. These reveal latent possibilities which may or may not come into practice. For example, you might have a terrifying dream of a nasty childhood experience. That dream, like the experience it symbolizes, is a part of your psychological makeup. It will influence you to some degree, perhaps in a limited way by scaring you and fixing it in your memory. But if the dream and its underlying motivation are powerful enough, they can exert influence on your behavior, either consciously or unconsciously. However, a scientist would say that the complex of psychological and experiential factors underlying the dream cause the eventual behavior, rather than giving the dream itself credit for behavioral changes. The dream, in other words, is a symptom rather than a cause.

There is another kind of dream which is a "symptom," one that often seems to predict illness. People will report dreams of pain, sometime to the extraordinary degree that they find the pressure of the edge of their bed is agonizing. Often, these dreams are followed by illness. French psychologists term them *rêves prémonitoires,* but do not fully explain their cause. One possibility is that in the inception of an illness, before you are consciously aware of the symptoms, your more sensitive unconscious mind may sense them and telegraph the news through a dream of pain or illness.

Our bodily health greatly influences our dreams. We all know of nightmares that follow on too much rich food, or the nocturnal fantasies that accompany a fever. The relationship between the state of our health and our dreams is so close that we should hesitate to put too much stock in something that depends on our digestion. Would your dream life be the same if you took an Alka-Seltzer before retiring? Probably not.

Because of the delicate interplay between the conscious and the unconscious mind during and just before sleep, our nocturnal imagery can be a source of creativity. We have an expression when a problem is before us that, "We will sleep on it." Researchers into creativity tell us that when the subconscious has free play—such as during sleep—we are susceptible to fresh solutions for our problems, or a release of poetic capability. Karl Gauss discovered his laws of induction in a dream, Paul Ehrlich came upon his side-chain theory through a nocturnal image. Niels Bohr developed his vision of an atomic model while sleeping. In 1865, the chemist Friedrich August Kekulé von Stradonitz solved the problem of the benzene ring, so important to modern chemistry, in a similar way. Kekulé dreamed of Ouroboros, the tail-biting serpent who figures prominently in magical symbolism. Since Ouroboros bites his own tail, he forms a circle. When he woke up, Kekulé thought of atoms arranged in a ring—exactly the solution he sought.

Stranger still is the experience of the Assyriologist, Hermann Hilprecht. He was puzzling over the inscriptions on two pieces of agate which he found in the temple of Bel in Nippur. He had little success, until in a dream a Babylonian priest took him to this temple and explained the meaning of the inscriptions. The visiting priest also showed Hilprecht how to piece the stones together. When he woke up, the Assyriologist found out that his nocturnal information was correct. Scientifically explained, this would be a particularly vivid example of the subconscious, in which Hilprecht may have had his solution, bringing its creative bundle to the conscious mind. If one is given to occult explanations, this is simply another clear case of a prophetic dream. In any case, our dreams do have meaning and purpose, even if they are not as clear as the dream books would have us believe. They don't predict the future in any direct way, but they do reveal a great deal about our subconscious activities. Dreams are a way to explore inner space. It is this area of dream study that fascinates scientists and intrigues many enthusiasts for dream interpretation. And they are only on the threshold of understanding the strange world of dream life.

The forms of divination we have looked at so far depend on some intermediary device—a number, a dream, an omen, or the like. There is another form of divination that depends solely upon the charismatic powers of an individual. This is intuitive prophecy. Miss Jeane Dixon is the best known of the modern intuitive prophets. In her books, she has made her revelations known to the general public. Her greatest fame came with her prediction of the tragic assassination of President John F. Kennedy in 1963. Her prophecies come as overwhelming intuitions, with such force in her mind that she attributes them to God. Miss Dixon is a very sensitive, fundamentally religious, extremely intuitive person. While everyone has intuitions, feelings, and premonitions, Jeane Dixon takes them seriously, firmly believing that they represent a higher truth that communicates to her through the faculty of intuition.

She makes a distinction between simple intuition and the special revelations which come to her as crystal-clear visions. Her anticipation of the Kennedy assassination was a visionary-type revelation, which she feels are the ones with utterly compelling power. Intuition, when intense, can manifest itself in the vivid clarity of a vision that appears like reality. It would be hard to make her distinction on a psychological basis, but Miss Dixon feels the differences are pronounced, from a psychic point of view. Her more visionary revelations are the ones which seem to happen and she feels, modestly, that God—or some divine being—uses her to reveal truth primarily through these special visions.

Most of us have been carefully schooled to mistrust our feelings. You can't run a business on feelings; they are too emotional; facts and figures are the staff of financial life. Our human relationships, when they are filled with intuition, feeling, and emotion, take on rich color, but at the same time they become very complicated; the cool rational approach to something like a marital argument is our norm for family relationships.

Women traditionally tend to rely more on feelings than men, and "subjective" personalities give feelings more credence than the more "objective" personality type. Actors and actresses, whose entire careers depend on the communication of and receptivity to deep emotional feeling, often display remarkable intuitive powers. Scientists still aren't certain about the feeling side of man's life.

Is an emotion, such as fear, simply a name given to a constellation of physical reactions, including clammy hands, sweating, and trembling limbs? Or is the emotion a thing-in-itself, something with an independent existence which is the cause of the physical reactions? This classic question in psychology still stumps the experts.

Whether you accept the validity of intuitive prophecy or not depends on whether you can believe that there is a Realm of Being that transcends this material world of time and space and from which communications can be established with persons in this plane of existence. There is no scientific evidence that this is so, naturally, but almost every major religion is based on the conviction that it can happen. Jesus, for example, is one who, in Christian thought, revealed the Heavenly Father. Buddha's followers do not believe he is the incarnation of the Supreme Being, but they hold that he broke through the line between the physical and spiritual worlds, and can show them the way to do the same.

If these great religious leaders are correct, then it is logical to assume that other people could have this same gift. However, believing something about a religious prophet centuries in the past and accepting the same thing about an ordinary mortal now living are two different things. Religions, especially Christianity, try to limit the points at which the Divine breaks through to the material realm, or else we would have theological chaos.

It is hard to prove the truth or falsity of intuitive prophets. Their source of insight—themselves—may have no causal connection with the events foretold, but we have more confidence in the human mind as a prognosticating instrument than we have in cards or sheep's livers. We have all had enough experience with intuition to believe in it, or at least to hesitate a long moment before we dismiss it. Further, when the prophecy is totally subjective, as an intuition is, one cannot sort out the actual intuition from the stock of facts in the prophet's mind which may combine, in more understandable ways, to suggest that something is going to happen. Intuitive prophets point out occasions on which they have predicted specifics that general good sense could hardly supply.

They also make a big point of their successes and overlook their failures. Miss Dixon's syndicated column for October 20,

1968 had to be withdrawn. In it, she said: "I still stand on my New Year's prediction and see no marriage for Jackie (Kennedy, now Onassis) in the near future." Her prediction of peace in Vietnam in 1965 has been carefully forgotten. Simply as a matter of percentages, some intuitive insights will come to pass. Human nature tends to overlook the failures and remember the successes, which may indicate a deep need in us all to believe that man can look into his future.

In the ancient world, the Delphic oracles had a reputation that spread over the whole civilization. The Greeks used a large number of these women who seemed to have special rapport with the gods, but the one at Delphi was without a peer. Greek mythology tells how Apollo slew the Python at Delphi, and as the dragon's body rotted underground, it gave off noxious gases. A cave at Delphi, where an underground stream ran and where the air was thought to be filled with terrible fumes, came to be known as the site of this struggle. The priestess who took up residence there drank from the stream, chewed laurel leaves, and sat on a tall tripod surrounded by snakes and enveloped with the supposed fumes of the cave. She went into a trance, offering enigmatic advice to the thousands of pilgrims who worked their way up the craggy cliffs to the cave of the great Oracle. The Pythia (priestess or oracle) had three apprentices in attendance, and this system kept the Delphic oracle business going as an institution for centuries.

We use the phrase "a Delphic answer," meaning a reply that is so ambiguous you can make it mean anything you wish. This is the literary style of the Delphic prophetesses. The most famous Delphic oracle is the one the Pythia returned to King Croesus of Lydia. The king sent messengers, asking whether or not he should go to war against the Persian Empire. The oracle replied:

> When Croesus shall o'er Halys river go
> He will a mighty kingdom overthrow.

Croesus found the advice reassuring and gathered his troops for the invasion. He crossed the Halys river and ran into trouble.

He not only lost the war, but his kingdom as well. He shrieked deception and went to Delphic oracles for the equivalent of his money back. The priestess simply smiled. The gods had told her a kingdom would fall, but they didn't say *which* kingdom.

A Pythia was holy, pure, removed from worldly cares. This special quality of removal from the world has seemed to be important for our oracles; when they are different, their advice seems more profound, more worthwhile. Rarely is a prophet an ordinary housewife. Even modern prophets, such as Miss Dixon, need to convey a quality of deep spirituality similar to the life of a devout mystic. A couple of instances are on record, however, when the Delphic oracle took a bribe to offer a special prophecy.

The Delphic Oracles and a host of lesser imitators continued a fertile existence until Christianity triumphed in the Roman Empire. Constantine took the sacred tripod from Delphi and removed it to his new city of Constantinople, where it still remains. His son, Constantius, instituted a widespread purge of all oracles, ruthlessly prosecuting them throughout the eastern Roman Empire.

But the intuitive prophet could not be stopped so simply, either by legal persecution or victorious Christianity. Before long, people with special prophetic gifts captured the respect and admiration of Europeans.

One of the most interesting of these is Nostradamus, who lived in the sixteenth century. You can find his book of prophecies in your public library, for he is read by thousands who claim that this extraordinary man predicted almost everything that is going to happen to the end of time.

Born Michel de Notredame in 1503 at San Remy, a town in southern France, he studied medicine and practiced as a physician until his middle years. Then he was "adopted" by Henri II and his wizard-loving queen, Catherine de Medici, who was a patron of all kinds of prophets. This royal sponsorship insured his fame.

Nostradamus specialized in political prophecy. He was an unparalleled necromancer, having correctly predicted the death of Henri II four years in advance. Henri's widow summoned Nostradamus and the two of them spent forty-five nights in séances, during which Nostradamus summoned up various angels and

63

paraded the images of her three sons across a mirror. Catherine's sons were destined to become kings of France, but in this apparition her own sons appeared only briefly while her son-in-law, the king of Navarre, appeared for a much longer time. This seemed to say that her own bloodline would have short reigns. Catherine, herself quite mystical, became so frightened that she urged Nostradamus to stop. As things turned out, Nostradamus was essentially correct and Catherine had a true glimpse into the future of her sons.

His major work, *Centuries,* contains about 1000 prophetic quatrains. They read like this sample:

> When litter overturned by the whirlwind,
> And faces will be covered by their coats,
> The republic, plagued by new people
> Then whites and red will judge contrarily.[2]

This is the classic ambiguity of a Delphic answer. He certainly makes no mention of specific people, of Hitler, Stalin or Roosevelt, although Nostradamians have claimed their prophet foresaw the rise of these men and the rearrangements of power in the twentieth century. Slippery language is basic to prophecy. For example, his followers tell us that Nostradamus foresaw the Great Fire in London of 1666. They point to this:

> The blood of the just at London will make mistake,
> Burnt by lightning of twenty three the six.[3]

The numbers in the original French are *vingt trois les six.* The faithful say this means 20 times 3 plus 6, or 66, to which they add another 1600 from somewhere, and come up with 1666. If you read the numerical reference as meaning 23 times 6, you have 138, which cannot be easily adapted to fit the required year of 1666. A prophecy means largely what the hearer or reader wishes it to mean.

---

2. Nostradamus, *Centuries* I. iv, in *Spirits, Stars, and Spells,* literally trans. Catherine C. and L. Sprague de Camp (New York: Canaveral Press, 1966).
3. Ibid., II. li.

A respectable number of Christians play the prophetic game with the Bible. They have a conviction the Holy Writ offers an outline for the future of mankind, especially in such visionary books as Daniel and the Revelation of St. John. Diffuse references to kingdoms, represented by beasts, can be applied to any existing power structures. The best biblical scholars conclude that these references point to the political situation at the time of the writing, and are simply literary and poetic devices used by the apocalyptic writers to make their point. Nonetheless, people continue to read them as messages for the future, although biblical prophecy has a record of being able to "show" how the Bible "predicts" the *present* state of affairs, while notoriously unable to come up with an accurate picture of the *next* decade.

Looking into the future still occupies man's mind. Sometimes exotic methods of prediction prove true, or so near to the truth that we can generously attribute some special insight to them. The laws of probability indicate that this will happen, especially if a prophecy is generally vague. There is no proof that intuitive prophets, or methods of divining the future, have any better records in the long run than what we would call educated guesses. The late columnist Drew Pearson was famous for his "predictions." He claimed he was right about eighty percent of the time, and he managed this feat without relying on supernatural resources. He was simply a canny observer of politics and a man of sound judgment. In order to be convincing, those who claim some esoteric means of prophecy will have to maintain a record of successes better than that achieved by intelligent observers and statistical predictors. Now and then, they manage to outdo the experts, but in the long haul they don't. A few lucky hits doesn't prove that prophecy is a reliable means of prediction. In any field as subjective as prophecy, you simply can't distinguish between what the prophet gets from "outside" sources and what he manages to find out with his own common sense.

A prophecy without a time limit—such as "one day Christ will return on earth and set up his Kingdom"—is always safe. It can still conceivably occur. "The power of the world, come the time of the dark clouds, goes from West to East" is a prophecy of the same kind. It suggests that the Eastern civilizations will one day dominate the world, a very likely possibility. The "time of the dark clouds" is sufficiently unspecific to avoid embarrassing time limits. It is quite another thing to predict in May 1970 that by October 1, 1973, the Peoples' Republic of China will invade Russia, achieving victory by spring of 1975, after which the Chinese will rule Russia and Eastern Europe. This is a very specific prediction and the time given for fulfillment is close enough to the actual prediction that those who hear it can remember when this big day comes. Prophets generally avoid anything this specific, because it is very risky.

One survey of Nostradamian prophecies as interpreted by his followers was made in 1950. It revealed that twenty interpreters offered 449 predictions based on the master's work. Forty-one have been fulfilled, 18 definitely failed, and 390 could still conceivably happen. On the surface, this is a good record. But all the false predictions had time limits on them, and among the prophecies without time limits, the record was two wrong to every one right, which is far below the 50-50 possibility of random chance. The successful prophecies and the 390 that could still come to pass were the sort of thing that anyone could expect to happen in human life some time or other. The key to testing prophecy, then, is insisting on verifiable time limits.[4]

When prophets who use the Bible to predict the future are tested in the same way, they usually fail. Everyone who has pinned down a specific date for Christ's glorious return to earth has proven wrong, although all historic Christian churches still indulge in the general prophecy that he will someday come back.

---

4. Nostradamus hit the nail right on the head with one of his prophecies (*Centuries* III. xcvi):
> Chief of Fossan will have throat cut
> By leader of the light and greyhound:
> The act gotten up by those of Tarpeian mount,
> Saturn in Leo thirteenth February.

On February 13, 1820, the duke of Berry (title: Lord of Fossano) was stabbed by a man who had been the royal houndsman. This is a singular example, and it amazes us. However, one good prediction out of a thousand such prophecies is not a convincing record, even though our amazement at even these kind of lucky hits gives us a sense of awe. We tend to believe, "If he was right once, he might be again." This psychological quirk is the mainstay of prophecy.

The church hasn't knocked future prediction directly. They use it themselves. Every denomination has a research office to predict trends in denominational and institutional life. Churches also proclaim a general picture of the end of history, drawn from certain biblical references to the final coming of Christ. A few, as we noted, use certain biblical passages in the same way Nostradamians use their prophet, as a source book of specific predictions. Generally, the Christian church has not endorsed occult prediction, although the Roman and Orthodox churches venerate saints whose chief contribution to mankind was an intuitive prophecy about a coming event. The basic need for magic among the Christian faithful leads them to use their saints and biblical writers as tools for divination, but the church has steered clear of endorsing this practice as a desirable act of piety.

But people who want to know what tomorrow will bring cannot be stopped by ecclesiastical pronouncements; they will find some way to baptize divination and carry it on under Christ's label. The Christian doctrine of providence teaches that man should trust in God who controls all things. In his almighty love, God will care for his children, who should patiently accept what comes their way as his inscrutable will. Human beings are simply less passive than this doctrine requires, so they still prophesy—by science or the occult—and try to outwit, or spy on, God's plans. When they don't like what he seems to have in mind, they take matters into their own hands. Political prophecy, such as Karl Marx indulged in, becomes self-fulfilling as soon as enough people believe that the prophet has truly outlined the inevitable course of future events. Not wishing to await God's pleasure, men construct their own maps of the future and proceed to follow their own paths toward their goals. ↗

4

That Old Black Magic Has Me in Its Spell

When we think of the word "occult," our mind easily forms pictures of witches dancing frenziedly about a fire in the darkness of deep woods. Or we might envision black magicians robed magnificently as they conduct obscene rites in a Black Mass dedicated to Satan. These pictures come too easily. The occult is a mixed bag, but only a relatively small part of the whole contemporary occult spectrum indulges in black magic. Yet our fascination with the seamy side of these esoteric arts goes on and on. Check your local library; chances are that in the occult section, books about witches and Satanism occupy a fair part of the shelf.

The reasons for our strange attraction to black magic aren't hard to figure out: it is weird, it offends every moral and social value we have inherited (thus providing a little middle-class rebellion), and it is very sexy in a twisted way. We all take perverse delight in the odd and unusual. If our sensibilities happen to be rigidly conventional, we won't go to a sideshow to gawk at the freaks, nor will we feel comfortable reading that journal of sex and oddities, the *National Enquirer,* on our morning commute to the office. But reading a book about witchcraft and black magic—at least in this moment when the subject has intellectual class—looks quite respectable.

That Old Black Magic Has Me in Its Spell

Black magic, unfortunately, is no longer purely a literary form of polite pornography and sadomasochism. Nor is it merely an interesting aberration in the distant past of man's hisotry. Black magic is alive and well—you can find it, in modern dress, being practiced in Los Angeles, New York, Philadelphia, London, and other major cities, along with rites in smaller communities. On the deranged fringes of the hippie subculture, we think we see frightening manifestations of a sinister power of darkness moving people to grossly outrageous deeds. The Manson family, implicated in the ghastly murders of actress Sharon Tate and her friends, appear, from evidence presented at their trial in Los Angeles, to have immersed themselves in an inverted morality of death and evil. Other murders in California, of the kind once perpetrated by sadistic psychopaths, have been connected with similar cultists.

The success of the film *Rosemary's Baby,* by the master of macabre films, Roman Polanski, which tells the classic black story of the Devil seeking a bride in a form of inverted Incarnation, shows how much we love this sort of thing. (Ironically, Mr. Polanski was the husband of Miss Tate, whose death brought evil from the screen to his home.) Drive-in theaters frequently run four feature-length horror films on one night to a packed lot. Even the skin flick producers cash in on the new trend toward the horrible. Some recent "art" films center about Black Mass ceremonies which, as we shall note later, provide ample material for the unusual needs of a double-X rated film maker.

It is easy, but really dishonest, to interpret black magic through the worst versions of it in today's news. Modern cultists of satanic power often caricature historic black magic. In fact, there is some historical doubt about the evidence we have on witchcraft and black magic: modern users of black arts may be adopting a symbol system that was manufactured by devoted Christian inquisitors to justify their persecutions of witches and devils. The only way to evaluate what now goes on under this label, without jumping to unsound conclusions, is to take a look at the history of black magic and witchcraft.

Magic is the source of most occult arts. Basically, magic is the art of manipulating the course of nature by supernatural means;

it is a system for controlling the existing order of things. Magic was man's earliest form of science. Both magic and science share the same fundamental aim—controlling nature. The scientist, of course, uses purely natural means in his methods of control.

Magic also has close associations with religion. As a matter of fact, no matter how enlightened and sophisticated one of the great religions becomes, elements of magic enter into it. Religion differs from magic mainly in that it seeks to *reverence* supernatural powers, while magic tries to *manipulate* them. Anyone familiar with a religion such as Christianity, as it is ordinarily practiced, knows that a lot of believers work hard to manipulate God for their own ends. How many prayers have been directed to God, asking him to avert a disaster, or bring rain? When Apollo 13 got into trouble on its moonward journey, the Congress of the United States called upon God to intervene in the natural course of events in order to insure the safe return of the astronauts. Technically, this is as much a magical act as the Roman *haruspices* sacrificing a pigeon to the gods for the safe return of a general from battle with the barbarians.

Even the most rational among us harbor streaks of the magical in our hearts, whether we openly admit it or hide our magic under a more acceptable label, perhaps by incorporating it into our respectable religion. We might speak of "white" magic, which is the gentle and harmless form of the art, and of "black" magic, which is the kind we don't happen to like for some reason.

That is actually how the adjective black happened to be applied to magic. In pre-Christian days, Western man simply used magic. He didn't see any point in making value judgments about its various forms, because magic was everywhere. When the church dominated European spiritual life in the Middle Ages, it stuck the pejorative term "black" on any form of magic which it did not sponsor, because the church at this time engaged in any number of odd magical practices designed to placate God and win his favor—from pilgrimages to holy places to the simple veneration of old bones and relics of saints.

Black magic, being so roundly denounced by the established church and its devotees hounded by the fiery tongs of the in-

70

quisitor, provided a convenient framework for someone who wished to rebel against the structures of the existing society. By the end of the Middle Ages, we find that parodies of the Christian faith entered into magical rites. The Black Mass, for example, is a tasteless caricature of the church's mass, which excites its worshipers primarily because it insults the establishment. Without a doubt, this motive plays a powerful role in the revival of black magic interest today. When one tires of insulting police, burning flags, and shouting obscenities in public, in order to dramatically spit out one's disgust with the established order, he can put on a Black Mass and engage in black magic to degrade the "God of Establishment Religion." Some early black magicians may have been primitive Yippies.

Magic has some basic principles. Sympathetic magic operates on the principle of analogy; that is, it performs a ceremony that imitates the desired end. For example, Amerindians on the North Pacific coast knew that sea shells can be very old, so rubbing a forehead with powdered sea shell imitates, by analogy, long life and brings this blessing to the receiver. A voodoo practitioner who puts pins in a doll to cause death or pain to his intended victim also works with analogy.

The famous scholar of mythology, Sir James Frazer, in his monumental work *The Golden Bough,* speaks of imitative magic —like produces like—and contagion magic—in which things which were once in contact continue a magical relationship, as a piece of a person's clothing carried with you can give you that person's vital force. (This is similar to our carrying pictures of our family in wallet or purse. Having the image with us represents the presence of the actual person.) Sigmund Freud, in *Totem and Taboo,* suggests that sympathetic magic rests on the wrong assumption made by primitive man that the world truly reflects his thought, a mix-up between one's mental state and reality.

Later anthropologists criticized Frazer by claiming that the acts of imitation in magic are really means of communication. They assert that these acts don't *in themselves* accomplish anything, but they do inform the supernatural powers about the magician's wishes.

Present-day magicians hold that the will of man is central to their art. As the late Aleister Crowley, a twentieth-century English magician, put it: "Magick (*sic*) is the Science and Art of Causing Change to occur in Conformity with Will." Even though they honor the ancient rituals, they explain that their efficacy doesn't depend on the ritual as much as upon the intensity of the magician's mental powers. This psychological explanation is more congenial to our times, for we believe in willpower. Faith healers, who might be called magicians under another name, realize full well the role of the will in effecting remarkable happenings.

We have the records of the ceremonial forms in which magic has been cast over the years. They come to us from many sources. Some ideas filtered through the pre-European civilizations of Mesopotamia, Egypt and Greece. Some derive from early European fertility rites. A few come from misinterpretations of Christian doctrine, and a lot come from imitations of church rites. But the Jewish mystical system of the Cabala supplied most of the content to ceremonial magic in the late Middle Ages.

The Cabala began early in the Middle Ages, chiefly as a spiritualizing counterforce to the prevailing orthodox Judaism which has become excessively rigid and legalistic. The Cabala began as a direct search for God, a quest for a personal encounter with him, apart from the complicated legal systems developed by the rabbis. Beginning as an oral tradition claiming its source in ancient times, the Cabala incorporated gnostic-like elements from the mysticism of Neoplatonism. It taught that God was the source of the world of the senses, but this objective world is the result of emanations from the divine source. There were twenty-two emanations and whether they represented the good or evil side of reality depended upon their relative distance from the source in God. In true Neoplatonic fashion, Cabala taught that man's soul existed from eternity and was independent of the body. In fact, the soul dwelling in flesh is a tragic misfortune, but if the soul is pure, it can overcome evil forces and foretell the future. So far, this resembles similar Neoplatonic systems that early Christian mystics used to undergird their quest for God.

Before long, the Cabala acquired magical qualities. Its teaching

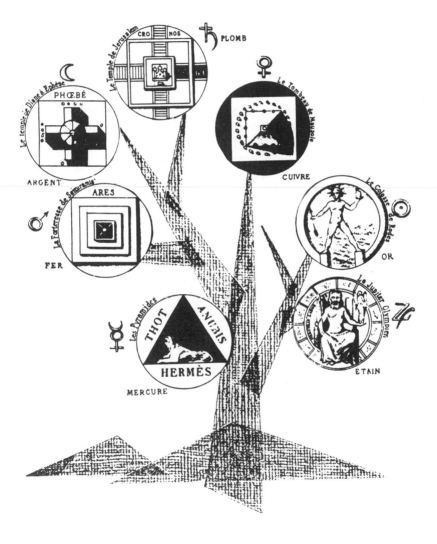

Magic, astrology, and alchemy blended into one medieval mix. This pictorial "Tree of Magic" illustrates how the various magical arts are related.

that the Scriptures contained mysterious, hidden meanings; its preoccupation with the symbolism of numbers and letters of the Hebrew alphabet and words invented from significant letter combinations—especially its connection of the twenty-two emanations with the twenty-two Hebrew letters, which related verbal activity with the force of divine power—helped the Cabala drift into magical use, even though it did not begin as a magic system. Christians, about the fifteenth century, became intrigued with cabalistic mysteries and this belief system, in a degenerate form, came into wide circulation.

Ceremonies deriving from cabalistic sources, mingled with Christian overtones, provided the bill of fare for magic during its golden age. Remnants of these ceremonies still survive. Most occult and theosophical orders adapt some of these old rituals in their own ceremonies. The rites of Freemasonry also incorporate elements that go back to this period.

Magicians themselves began to make a distinction between black and white magic. Black magic (goety) was exercised with the intention of harm. Handbooks for cursing and hexing were called grimoires, such as the *Grand Grimoire*. White magic, called theurgy, was performed to help people by casting off evil and aiding their lives. Both styles included making pacts with devils and demons, as well as prayers to the benevolent God of Christianity (or Judaism).

Magic is something more complex than a neat compact with the Devil. Magicians honored his diabolical presence, but they generally advised one to go as far as he could with God before finally resorting to the satanic kingdom. Magicians played both sides of the spiritual street. In a time when war, pestilence and famine regularly marched over the land, people didn't mind covering their bets when it came to dealing with the supernatural source of all these horrors. Our picture of Faust selling his soul to the Devil to gain powers is an oversimplified image of how magic operated.

The magician himself needed principles and strong character. Eliphas Levi, an occultist who collected a great deal of magic lore, said that traditionally the magus (magician) should be a man with much self-respect, living a methodical life sheltered from anything

74

or anyone he cannot esteem. He should feel that he is a dethroned sovereign awaiting the return of his crown. Another student of magic says that the chief requirement of a magician was to know the state of his own soul in relation to the power of the universe. This gives us a picture of a man who is proud, highly egotistical, self-centered, and extremely cool with a lot of self-control. These character traits were essential. Anyone lacking a firm grasp on his mind and total self-control could go insane dabbling in the terrifying mysteries of magic. A number of people did just that, to the point where the Jewish community banned the Cabala because it drove people crazy.

Magicians were often called upon to help out in love affairs. The relationship of magic and sex is rather close, perhaps because magic reacted against the church and the church did not think much of human passion. In any case, one of Louis XIV's mistresses, Mme. de Monespan, consulted a magician who performed spells and offered "amatory masses" to assist her in her competition with the other girls who sought royal favor.

Before performing any magic, the magus prepared and consecrated himself with more energy than a regular priest. His clothes had to be made of special material and covered with magical symbols such as the pentagram, or five-pointed star. His wand and other instruments were prepared according to specific instructions, including the proper time of night and moon phase in which the limb used for a wand could be cut. The magician also engaged in a time of personal preparation, consecrating himself to his task as priests of the gods have done since the beginning of history. The *Grand Grimoire* gives instructions for his personal preparation:

You must abstain during an entire quarter of the moon from the society of females, so as to protect yourself from the possibility of impurity. You must commence your magical quarter at the same moment with that of the luminary itself by a pledge to the Grand Adonay, who is Master of all Spirits, and make no more than two collarions (light meals) daily . . . using the following prayer previously to each repast during the whole of the said quarter:

Prayer

I implore Thee, Thou Grand and Powerful Adonay, Master of all Spirits! I beseech Thee, O *Elohim,* I give unto Thee my soul, my heart, my inward parts, my hands, my feet, my desires, my entire being! O Grand Adonay, deign to be favorable unto me! So be it—Amen.

The use of the Hebrew Old Testament names for God—*Adonai* and *Elohim*—reflects the Jewish cabalistic influence. The proper name for God—Yahweh—was considered too magical to be spoken aloud and remained a magical tetragrammaton, YHWH.

The magician worked within the magic circle. The circle probably derives from the old Greek notion that the perfect and divine geometrical shape was circular. A circle was drawn, usually nine feet in diameter, often with another circle just inside or outside of the main one. This would be decorated with stars and other symbols, formed with mace, lined with candles, and painted with equilateral triangles. A chalk circle suited white magic while evil spells required a black circle. Drawing the circle completed the magician's preparations. He would conduct his rites from within it, as it protected him from impure spirits. The circle became so identified with magic that when the witch-hunts began in earnest, anyone who aimlessly drew a circle in the dirt with a stick risked arrest and trial as a witch.

A magician may or may not have included a Black Mass in the magical ritual. It depended on the practitioner. Often, defrocked priests or ordained degenerates would be called in for this part of the action, to add a touch of irony. A Black Mass is really uncomplicated. One simply does everything possible to blaspheme the regular mass. Invert the crucifix, substitute "evil" for "good," "Satan" for "God," recite the mass backwards, and pledge your soul to the Devil. Deviant sexual practices are often added.

Some scholars think this kind of ecclesiastical parody is an early form of protest movement. Certainly this could be true. Most of those who would enjoy such a thing would have to be nominal Catholics who intensely despised the church or its creed. But there is evidence that such masses were actually offered in honor of

Satan, to worship him as against the God of Christianity. Some groups thought Lucifer was wrongly cast from heaven by God, and felt he was the true ruler of the universe. This may be traced to the church's attack on cherished "old religion" traditions. During the Black Plague, for example, one can readily imagine terrified people, tormented by fears that God had deserted the world, turning to Satan worship as the logical next step to rid themselves of the dread plague. Black Masses were used especially in magic ceremonies designed to gain a lover—the "amatory masses" that Mme. de Montespan tried—or to kill an enemy. The connection between love and death in this instance has intriguing philosophical implications! The writings of de Sade illuminate this paradoxical relationship.

Practitioners of formal, ceremonial magic derived from the Cabala and other sources represent the priestly caste of magic. They are usually males. Witches represent the popular expressions of the art. And they are usually females. Witchcraft and magic became very confused as they twisted together over the years into one braid. Each seeks the same goals and has the same basic philosophy, but the two can be distinguished by the way in which they were practiced. Present-day witches claim magic powers, but there are also magicians who refuse to be called witches. The distinction might be loosely explained this way: witchcraft is a popular magic that draws upon the rites of the old religions, while magicians seem more "scholarly," basing their art on a self-conscious philosophy and devoting a lot of time to personal preparation. A magus might compare with a Catholic priest, while a witch parallels Wesleyan revivalists. Magic is cooler, less emotional than witchcraft. In normal usage, the words magic and witchcraft are used interchangeably, even though this may not be strictly correct.

In the hinterlands of medieval Europe, which means anywhere beyond the city limits, fragments of the pre-Christian religion survived in the popular mind, especially in northern Europe. A horned god appears in many of these ancient cults, probably a distorted leftover of the ancient animal gods. This god usually appears as a he-goat, or a bull, but he could take any animal form, such as a dog or cat. When the peasants met secretly to indulge in their old rites, but couldn't spare an animal to represent this god, a man dressed in dark robes served the purpose.

The witches' horned god is totally distinct from the Devil of Christian tradition, but it influenced the church's imagery of the Devil. Witness our most popular way of drawing a devil: an animal-like creature with horns. As priests and missionaries moved through the reaches of Europe with the new religion, they found themselves condemning the old pagan gods as representatives of the anti-Christ or satanic forces. Consequently, the ceremonies we call witchcraft came to be termed devil worship. As Christian religious symbols captured the imagination of the masses of people, and the number who indulged in the old rites shrank into a small minority, the old religion picked up some ideas and images from Christianity and, being more of an aberration than a dominant religious force, opened itself to persecution by the now well-entrenched Christian church. The practitioners of witchcraft began to forget about the old gods and thought of themselves as devil worshipers, just as the church had taught them.

Eventually, the church reached the point where it stopped playing games with pagan ideas by "baptizing" the old ceremonies into the faith and began to set up stakes, gather faggots, hire inquisitors as it set out earnestly to rid the Christian world once and for all of this so-called devil worship.[1]

Witchcraft is a word that describes a form of religion that incorporates men and nature in a harmonious manner unknown to the scientific Western man. It is still practiced in Africa, the Pacific Islands—any place where the influences of our civilized separation of man and nature have not penetrated. As Pennethrone Hughes observes: "Witchcraft is the degeneration of one

---

1. However, by this time the old pagan fears had also crept into the liturgy of the church. Exorcism—the casting out of evil spirits—was a function of a Catholic priest as well as a magician. Liturgies for baptism still contain elements of exorcism. The liturgical form for entering a new church building usually includes having the priest rap on the door a few times before the congregation makes their initial entrance. Originally, this little ceremony was devised to exorcise evil spirits lurking in the yet unconsecrated building. Church furnishings, especially the holy objects, receive special consecration, a rite that probably originated in pagan fears about impure spirits.

of the earliest stages of religious belief and practice. In its history it had added parodies of the various later religions which have challenged it, and which, after generations of struggle, have usually swamped it. The story of the witch cult is only comprehensible against the background of religious development as a whole."[2]

Our image of witches comes to us from the three hags in *Macbeth,* stirring their filthy cauldrons and muttering weird chants; from Grimm's *Fairy Tales,* where the long crooked fingers point their warts at you while the witch cackles; and from the late Walt Disney who filled our eyes with such monstrous females in his cartoon films. The truth is less unattractive; some witches were charming young women. Male witches (warlocks) are more rare; the kind of frenzied activity and hysteria associated with witchcraft seems more suited to susceptible females. One advocate of the Women's Lib movement mentioned to me that the whole witch business might have been a male chauvinistic plot to put down women.

European witches—and the American witches who come from the same roots—followed certain forms of organization and ritual which have come down to us from ancient reports. Witches organized into covens of thirteen. A male led a group of twelve females, and sometimes he impersonated or represented the Devil. Covens gathered periodically (usually monthly) for secret meetnigs called Sabbats. Certain very special gatherings, called Grand Sabbats, honored important days: The biggest holidays were All Hallows Eve (Halloween), and May Day. Other important days were Candlemas (February 2), Lammas (August 1), St. Thomas Day (December 1), the Eve of St. John (June 23), and Good Friday. They also met on the solstices and equinoxes. Notice that many of these days have Christian liturgical names, but this is misleading. Except for Good Friday, all of these dates were formerly days of pagan festivities, which the church had earlier incorporated into its liturgical calendar under Christian labels.

Witches met not only in the deep, dark woods, they also gathered at crossroads, fields, around special stones (especially where

2. Pennethrone Hughes, *Witchcraft* (Baltimore: Penguin Books, 1952), p. 21.

the sacred stone idea survived), or even in churchyards. They began proceedings at midnight, ending them with the first flush of dawn's light. Naturally, they traveled to the Sabbats on broomsticks or disguised as animals. A few less dramatic witches simply walked. A few would fly like birds after rubbing themselves with special ointments, gleefully shouting "Thout, thout, a tout, tout, throughout and about." Formulas for these ointments usually include belladonna, which is a hallucinating drug that could send one off on a mental flight, at least.

Once at the Sabbat, they followed a "liturgy of evil." First, they paid homage to the Devil, usually in the form of the *Osculum Infame,* or kissing Satan's (the male leader dressed in an animal costume) behind. Next, they went into a wild orgy of dancing, back-to-back and in a circle. Sometimes they leapt through a dance, similar to the Italian LaVolta, or did follow-the-leader steps. Then came the moment of copulation with the Devil. If the male leader didn't have the energy to service all the women, they might use other males present in the group. Satanic intercourse was considered cold and impersonal, and no children could issue except by mutual consent. This suggests they might have used an artificial phallus. Then, all the witches and warlocks would have a feast. After dinner (some reports have dead bodies as the main dish), new witches would receive initiation into the cult, by putting one hand on her head and another on her feet while pledging to the Devil all in between. After this, the covens would hear reports of magic and hear instruction in new developments in the black arts. The routine ended with a religious ceremony of some kind. It could be an animal sacrifice in the pagan style, or it could be a Black Mass. In the latter case, the mass was used to bewitch the Christian God, whom witches felt was cruel and evil.

Now, the question is, how do we know all this fascinating information? From unimpeachable sources—the witches themselves. During the witch-hunts conducted by Christ's holy church, suspected witches were interrogated in an effective manner that included hot tongs, pressing with stones, the rack, boiling water, Iron Maidens, and other tongue-loosening devices. As inquisitors asked questions, the terrified and agonized women poured forth answers that came to fill volumes of ecclesiastical trial reports.

Those nonjudicial reports of witch activity that we have usually tell what *one man* saw while he walked in the woods in the dead of night, or what he saw the neighbor lady do in the secrets of her chamber. It seems logical that if witches gathered in huge Sabbat meetings, some enterprising sheriff would have gathered some stout men and raided one and brought the whole lot of possessed women to prison for trial. Unfortunately, this never happened, so we have only the mass of evidence extracted under hideous torture. No written witch literature has come down from the Middle Ages, although we have magical books from this period.

This leaves one with the impression that the whole scheme of witch life actually originated in the minds of clerics and received tortured affirmation from "witches" as they gasped a panicked "Yes, yes, yes" when the hot iron passed in front of their eyes. No one doubts that old religious rites went on during the Middle Ages; they still happen now and then. But this is a far cry from the reports of organized witchcraft that have come down to us, especially in the flamboyant words of Romantic poets and writers.

The recorded stories told by alleged witches seem remarkably uniform. This consistency could be attributed to the real truth that underlies all the confessions. But we also know that if interrogators pursue a consistent line of questioning, that is, if they know already what they want their victim to confess, they come up with very consistent evidence. The Communist scare that rocked the United States under Senator Joseph McCarthy's leadership produced the same uniform evidence of a vast Red conspiracy. The conspiracy, in the form presented to the public, turned out to exist mostly in the fantasies of Senate investigators, whose questions were carefully phrased to bring forth the answers they already had in mind. No wonder this scourge got the name of witch-hunt.

Professor Margaret Murray, a noted Egyptologist, did the first extensive research into witchcraft, which she published in 1921. She realized that witchcraft formed a surviving remnant of old fertility beliefs, but she asserted that this religion was indeed widespread and well organized. She thought we should take the evidence extracted in the witch trials with some seriousness, and cautioned against disbelief as strongly as she warned against overly credulous belief. The question of how widespread and organized this counterreligion was still remains in doubt, as does the documentation from which we get our information. The only certain thing is that one way or the other a symbol system called witchcraft has entered into our mythology and some people today find it charming, even worthwhile.

Professor Murray's cautious view of a vast conspiracy of evil seems to imply that any religion of Satan so well organized would have written something down, or managed to get together in active resistance to the ecclesiastical witch-hunters. The impression from history is that the church picked off hapless victims one by one, because they were alone, scared, and didn't know what the fuss was all about. The orthodox Catholic view goes one giant step beyond Professor Murray's suggestions. This view holds that the Devil is real, his worshipers are real, and that witchcraft together with the other black arts truly represents the conspiratorial actions of the anti-Christ.

Modern witches do exist. *Life* magazine reported that some three hundred (mostly "white" witches) live in Greenwich Village alone, and they printed a picture of one with her face carefully hidden. Sybil Leek openly proclaims her adherence to witchcraft. She wrote about her life in the brisk selling biography, *Diary of a Witch.* She claims to know hundreds of witches, some of them well placed in society. Reliable reports, in such trustworthy sources as the *New York Times,* describe modern Sabbats going on in big cities among intelligent, seemingly respectable people. In my investigations I could not uncover anyone claiming to be a witch whom I trusted as being at least serious about the craft. Friends in whom I have confidence have told me about such people, however. These witches become such by conscious decision, but in the United States you can find places here and there where "authentic," or traditional, witchcraft is still practiced as it has been for centuries.

One location is the Dutch country of Pennsylvania, where witch-craft of the central European tradition is so vigorous a few witches have taken to openly hanging out their shingles. The German background farmers in the lush York and Lancaster counties of that state consult witches for wart removal and to help their hens lay more eggs and their cows give more milk. Some witches deal in black curses, and the fear of bewitchment runs as rampant among these sturdy farm folk as the Evil Eye terror dominates some Italian neighborhoods. Sometimes, witchcraft leads to vio-lence. Arthur Lewis's book, *Hex,* describes the story of a Dutch country murder trial of 1929. The charge on the books was mur-der and robbery, but witchcraft lurked in the background. The victim fell at the hands of men who thought he had bewitched them and when he refused to remove the curse, they killed him.

Understandably, the good people of Lancaster and York coun-ties are a bit hesitant to admit this prevalence of witchcraft. Lewis has said, only half in jest, that in these counties you could never convict a witch for the simple reason that you couldn't find a dozen people for a jury who weren't terrified of witchpower and black art reprisals.

However, almost anyone can become a witch. It is more a mat-ter of decision than heritage. And, I might add, witches today are mostly white, or good, witches. Sibyl Leek says, "People are search-ing for a religion where they don't have to live a godlike life, a religion that acknowledges them as human beings." She adds that witchcraft involves commitment: "I did not just wake up one morning and discover I was a witch. Witchcraft, like any other religion, must be accepted consciously. It is a decision that re-quires maturity."

A modern coven—and if your town has over 100,000 in-habitants, chances are a coven or two or more meets regularly—in England or the United States likely consists of six males and six females, preferably close to each other, such as married or engaged couples. The leader, number thirteen, is usually a woman. They may conduct their rites in the nude, which is one hang-over from fertility rites. The leader reads from the witches' bible, the *Book of Shadows.* They draw the nine-foot magic circle and gather in it for magic, only magic now has become an exercise in group will. A number of reporters claim that a good sex orgy follows the ceremonies. The picture this brings to mind is one of a suburban wife-swapping club with mystical overtones, but the satisfactions devotees get from it goes deeper than the excitement of mischievous sexual behavior in defiance of conventional morality. The modern cult is probably far more pedestrian and less lurid in its rites than the historic accounts of a witches' Sabbat.

There are, however, some examples of an outright rejection of established Western religion and its God in favor of an open commitment to Satan, the negation of the Christian God. A few years ago, Anton Szandor LaVey organized his First Satanic Church in a black-painted, Victorian style house in San Francisco. Soon, satellite congregations formed in other cities, Detroit and Toledo among them. LaVey has his own *Satanic Bible*. He devotes his cult to sensual indulgence, vengeance and sin of every sort. The San Francisco operation sports a dimly lit room, with black walls and red ceiling. A nude priestess reclines on the "altar" during services. LaVey makes no pretense about being a "good" magician or witch. He goes all the way for evil. He warns that "The one and only deadly sin in Satanism is self-deceit. Those who pussyfoot around are setting themselves up for bad news—using the Devil's tools but not giving the Devil his due." Services at the Church of Satan follow the traditional Black Mass.

At the root, LaVey's brand of Satanism represents an organized rejection of all conventional morality and religion. He has completely "transvalued all values" and proclaims the supreme rule of evil as the ultimate "Good" in the world. Worship of "Satan" is a symbolic expression of this rejection, for in the mythology of Western society Satan personifies all counterforces to good as normally understood. LaVey is not a profound philosopher, but this idea has a long philosophical history.

The infamous Marquis de Sade, in his often repressed and banned writings, argued that conventional morality was a fraud. The only real drive in man was what moralists call evil—the satisfaction of all one's lusts. He spoke of man as the supreme arbiter of his own morality, above reproach and condemnation. The characters in his novels dissipate themselves through brutality and end-less orgies. They release their perverted lusts behind high walls, in castles protected by several moats, in monasteries so high on a hill that no one comes near.[3] This isolated splendor accents the loneliness of moral judgment, when one is his own judge. De Sade himself did not escape punishment for his own efforts to live out his philosophy. Locked in prison, he dreamed of a world in which one would be free to do as he pleased, indulging all his human, sensual desires.

Recently, de Sade, long dismissed as the archetype of the pleasure in pain perversion, sadism, which was named after him, has been resurrected. Existentialists, especially, have given serious attention to his thought. His themes of a man whose morality transcends all existing morality, of man alienated totally from the world, of man who makes a transcendent moral decision, and therefore, in a real sense, cannot be held responsible for his actions by other judges, speak to the modern world—particularly if his ideas are separated from the sadistic sexual framework in which he wrote and are generalized to morality as a whole.

Viewed this way, de Sade profoundly anticipated the Nietzschean idea of a superman. Both thinkers penetrated deeply into the irrational depths of man's being and, in different ways, affirmed the potency of life fully lived, as opposed to moral systems that delay rewards to some vague future date. Nietzsche felt Christianity taught men how to die rather than how to live. The true will of man must draw upon all those human drives and potentialities that traditional morality condemns, in order that he might rise above accepted good and evil to destroy decadence. Symbolically con-sidered, that is, naming the total rejection of morals as Lucifer's action, this could be called Satanism. Adolph Hitler found inspira-tion in these writers, but so do other people whose ultimate vision

---

3. De Sade's isolated fortresses of evil are reflected in instructions to black magicians. A medieval grimoire, *Key of Solomon,* tells the magus: "The places best fitted for exercising and accomplishing Magical Arts and Opera-tions are those that are concealed, removed and separated from the habita-tions of men; wherefore, desolate and uninhabited regions are most appro-priate . . ." (quoted in Harry Wedeck, *Treasury of Witchcraft* [New York: Philosophical Library, 1961], p. 153).

of a strong society is much different from that of the German dictator.

Satanism of this kind remains a miniscule part of the universe of black magic. Most of what we call devil worship looks more like a simple rejection of the Christianity that imbues our culture. Witchcraft falls into this category, and contemporary magicians, like their cabalistic forebears, are also experimenting with a different religion. It is not a new religion; indeed, it goes back far beyond Christianity to the Stone Age, but it is a religion nevertheless. The question that haunts those of us schooled in the rationalistic thought forms of our times is, why would anyone dissatisfied with the Judeo-Christian tradition go back to almost prehistorical religious forms?

Partly, the answer lies in the recent revival of Romanticism, and its concomitant desire to weld man and nature into a comprehensive whole. Romanticism is fundamentally negative toward scientific modes of thought. It also enjoys dabbling in weird and far out ideas. The nineteenth-century burst of Romanticism brought us nature-mysticism, sensual poems—and the literature on witchcraft which we now consult.

In the thirties and forties, a group of expatriate British writers living in Southern California, numbering among them Aldous Huxley and Gerald Heard, explored human consciousness. They believed that man originally had a great sensitivity for "the other" and, in the course of developing his logical faculties, lost it. It appears in a debased form among certain "savage" tribes today, but Western man must recover it through deliberate effort. This led Huxley and Heard to Yoga and mystery religions.

They thought witchcraft was a fertility rite, but also thought it was an organized system which, through women, carried on the fight against the prevailing materialism of modern civilization in the West. The witches' Sabbats seen this way became escapist fantasies, when the joy within man bursts forth despite the penitential quality of the times. Magic performs the same function, by giving man and human nature a close, manipulative relationship with nature. In other words, magic and witchcraft are disguised forms of mysticism. The history of the Cabala—beginning as mystery and turning into magic—becomes reversed in our day.

There is an enormous amount of truth in this judgment, as we will see later. The church can respond best to the challenge of magic and witchcraft by reexamining its own mystical resources. Unfortunately, the orthodox Christian position is that the Devil is real and those who call upon his name are heretics. This makes it simple to condemn followers of magic, without trying to see what they really strive for.

Besides the religious bias against magic and witchcraft, we still have enough rationalism to laugh it all off as some kind of psychological aberration, which it partly is.

This is too bad. A serious look at what many of the rising number of magic devotees seem to look for might lead the church back to its own inner spiritual resources. Within its message, there is plenty of what these people seek: union with God and his creation. The church has a healthy path in this direction and should cut away the brush so people can see it clearly. Otherwise, they will go to cults with potentially dangerous mental consequences. As the old magicians said, "Try God first before turning to the Devil." It will be a shame if the church makes this impossible and forces sincere people to try the "Devil" first, quite possibly with great harm to their mental and spiritual health. ⊇

The Many-sided Psychic World

Those who can't stomach magical or supernatural explanations of strange phenomena—intuition, precognition, and the like—enjoy exploring the natural, scientific interpretations drawn from psychology: "His wife didn't come to him in a dream. The dream merely visualized his repressed wishes. When she left him for another man, as she said she was doing in the dream, this resulted only from his unconscious actions, or his subconscious awareness that she was about to leave him, although he could not consciously face the fact." When you think about it, such an explanation is as strange to common sense as the easier alternative suggestion that the occurrences have a supernatural source.

Nevertheless, these psychological theories hold more credence with the average person than ideas which drag in the supernatural. We are so conditioned to respect science, prone to demythologize everything, that we overlook the fact that sometimes the scientific approach takes us as far into the realm of fantasy as any other approach. However far we must go, most of us want to get rid of that notion "spirit." But when researchers probe into the workings of the mind, their results are startling and their theoretical interpretations go far beyond the classic "cause-effect" of traditional physics.

The power of the human mind astounds us. Many phenomena reported in traditional lore—clairvoyance, telepathy, communication with other spheres of existence, automatic writing—have caught scientific attention. Some researchers wonder if these strange experiences, even though misinterpreted and clouded over with legend, might not give clues to long overlooked human mental capacities. Scientific men who work from the premise that hidden and seemingly eternal myths, representing some identifiable force or mental capacity, might be uncovered have a tough road to travel. Science has erected its own orthodoxy and neatly classified, sometimes presumptuously, what is true and worthy of research, and what is plain nonsense.

Through the efforts of some courageous pioneers, this prejudicial attitude is starting to dissolve, at least in the area of psychological research. Our excitement with our own inner potential has unleashed a furious interest in areas that have long been on the "lunatic fringe" of psychology.

One of these areas is parapsychological research—the study of psychological activity that does not fit into the normal categories of the discipline. The general term used for these manifestations is *psi* processes, after the first letter in the Greek word, *psyche* or soul. The most familiar branch of this new study is known in the United States as ESP or extrasensory perception.

Dr. J. B. Rhine is the most notable name among the early pioneers. He has worked at Duke University and his operation there has now expanded into the Foundation for Research on the Nature of Man (FRNM).

He began his work in 1927, trying to control experiments in such a way that the validity of *psi* phenomena could be finally and certainly established one way or the other. Duke University, perhaps alone among American colleges, was receptive to this kind of program because of President Few's own interests. The late twenties were awash in an uncontrolled, often overly credulous wave of communication with the departed, hypnotism, and other strange activities that classic psychology couldn't explain. Dr. Rhine himself was drawn to the subject by his fascination with the classic "survival problem": Does life continue after death?

A researcher doing thesis work at Duke had made careful studies of a number of séances. He used "token sittings," in which the sitter, or inquirer, is not himself present, but is represented by a stenographer and a token object. This eliminated any chance for the medium to gain some possible information from the sitter's visible reactions. Careful studies of the transcripts convinced the Duke University psychology department, including the famous William McDougall, that the information given by the mediums checked could not be explained without hypothesizing some source of information from beyond the medium. How could this extra-sensory perception, which seemed necessary to explain the evidence, come about?

Dr. Rhine set to work on this problem, by testing telepathy (communication from one mind to another without the channels of senses) and clairvoyance (the power to discern objects or events not present to the senses).

He began with clairvoyance. He used Zener cards. These are five cards, each bearing one of these symbols: a circle, a plus sign, a rectangle, a star, and wavy lines. Using neutral symbols instead

Zener cards use these symbols in ESP experiments because they are neutral and unemotional.

of words removes any possible choices based on affection for a particular word. The subject is seated in a room and the experimenter moves to another room where he cannot communicate with the subject. The subject is asked to predict a series of five cards or more. The experimenter then checks his results. In a pack of twenty-five Zener cards, there are five sets of five symbols. The random chance of describing the position of a given card (like "the wavy line is above the star") is, in the long run, one in five.

ESP and Zener cards are a parlor game today, but in the laboratory it is a serious, carefully controlled, business.

Dr. Rhine finally found a subject, H. P., who achieved remarkable clairvoyant results. Once he achieved results with odds against chance amounting to 10^{20}. In a series of three hundred tests when he was in a room one hundred yards from the cards, H. P. made twice as many "hits" as chance would suggest. The odds against this happening are tremendous, so Dr. Rhine and his associates published a monograph on their findings in 1934.

While Dr. Rhine had better results with clairvoyant experiments, his contemporary in England, Dr. S. G. Soal, achieved his greatest success with telepathy. These experiments are harder to control because once a target is recorded, the receiver may clairvoyantly read it. Eventually a clear test for telepathy was developed. Dr. Soal found two subjects with remarkable abilities in this field, who could achieve results on the order of 10^{70} to 1 better than chance.

The team of researchers at Duke turned their attention to psychokinesis (PK), which is the influence of thought on the movement of objects. In their experiments, the parapsychologists used dice which were shaken and dropped by impersonal mechanical devices. Certain subjects could influence the movements of the dice with better than chance results, as any dedicated crapshooter is convinced he can do.

None of these experiments get down to the nitty-gritty questions that intrigue laymen: Can mediums communicate with the dead? Can dreams prophesy the future? Can substantial thoughts—instead of mere symbols—be transmitted telepathically? Can clairvoyants perceive the future course of a person's life?

These questions go far beyond the capabilities of the tools now used in parapsychological research. These workers have stuck with experiments based on games, because these are statistical, and they can be mathematically checked against chance results. But even this cautious, limited work has not impressed the majority of psychologists, who dismiss *psi* with a yawn. Although the number of professionals interested in parapsychology is growing, it is still the black sheep of the psychological sciences, too unorthodox for most universities to touch.

Research still goes on in *psi* processes, but the results of ESP research to date can be summarized briefly:

1. *Paranormal phenomena such as telepathy and clairvoyance do in fact exist.* The parapsychologists' reports of some experiments that show slim margins over chance expectations cause their colleagues to raise critical eyebrows. But this does not affect this general conclusion. Enough experiments have been so fantastically above chance that the *psi* processes, in some individuals, can be firmly established as real. However, and this is important, *only the behaviors studied in the laboratory* have been proven to this extent. ESP in relation to Zener card guesses, for instance, is demonstrable and repeatable, but this does not in any way permit clairvoyants looking into your future or mediums speaking with your dead aunt to claim laboratory proof. PK still awaits as certain a validation as these two *psi* processes.

2. *ESP abilities vary among individuals.* Some people have little or no capacity for the task. Professional mediums and clairvoyants, along with people who sense they have psychic powers, do not score any higher on the tests than the population as a whole. Children, however, have a markedly greater ESP ability than adults. Dr. Rhine and his associates theorize that this is due to the training we receive. Assuming that our schooling in the logical use of our faculties stunts our natural receptivity to ESP and that children are more "pure," closer to true human nature than adults, he concludes that the gift may belong to everybody, but most adults have lost it. This corroborates the neo-consciousness theories of Aldous Huxley and Gerald Heard, which we discussed in the last chapter.

3. *The mental condition of the subject affects his ESP abilities.* Boredom, disinterest, distrust of the experimenter, and anxiety can adversely affect the performance of a good ESP subject. Physical condition seems to have little or no effect. As far as intelligence is concerned, brighter people tend to have better ESP capabilities.

4. *The agent influences results. Psi* subjects can show greater results with one agent than with another.

5. *Space and time do not affect* PSI *results.* Card tests with people separated by thousands of miles work as well or better than when the agent and subject occupy the same building.

6. *The* PSI *processes seem to be in the unconscious part of personality.* Subjects who do not know whether they are successful or not do as well as those who are told of their progress.

7. *Drugs do not seem to increase* PSI *capacity.* There is no hope for a fast chemical way to become an instant psychic. However, some subjects under hypnosis or who have consumed moderate amounts of alcohol do better than when they are in their normal state. This may be due to the influence of the mental condition of the subject, for hypnosis and alcohol relax people considerably.

8. *Abnormality and subnormality do not affect results.* Institutionalized mental patients do no worse and no better in *psi* testing than people off the street.

This, generally, is the bulk of the relatively well-established scientific knowledge about *psi* phenomena. We certainly cannot take this meager information and generalize from it to the conclusion that the whole bag of psychic manifestations are definitely proven. Controlled laboratory work involves much simpler things than actual psychic happenings. Some psychiatrists and parapsychologists may claim this list is too conservative, but it does represent the major laboratory findings in the subject so far.

Like other occult arts, the psychic flourished three decades ago. Mediums appeared generally in the 1920s, when Arthur Conan Doyle and the famed Houdini carried on their vigorous debate over spiritualism. At the time, most mediums were demonstrable frauds. The new interest in the psychic is far more serious. Perhaps under the influence of such parapsychologists as Dr. Rhine, psychic research is taking a more scientific turn. There is a mood of caution, as was exemplified by Bishop Pike, and a strong desire to eliminate the frauds so that the subject can be explored without deception. This doesn't prove it is true, but it does show that people place greater hope in the psychic now than they did before. It is serious business because, as we shall see, it has profound religious implications.

Spiritualism, the communication of the dead with the living, began as an earnest study in the late nineteenth century. This was its great moment for birth for two reasons.

First, Darwin had recently published his work on evolution and a lot of people resented being shoved off into the primate column.

They sought a viewpoint that put man back on center stage, and spiritualism seemed like a good option.

Second, the matter of survival of human life beyond death became a problem at this time. Prior to this, most people either assumed immortality or eternal life, or else they kept their mouths shut. By the end of the nineteenth century, science and materialistic philosophy had spread wide doubts about the continuation of life. Religious believers and humanists alike sought some quasi-scientific evidences that would reinforce the belief, or prove conclusively, that life goes on beyond the grave. Communication with the departed seemed like the right place to start. Early psychical research attracted such luminaries as psychologist William James and philosopher Henry Sedgwick.

The new quest caught the passionate interest of the masses. They, too, were looking for some affirmation of spirituality in an age of materialism and scientific "arrogance." By the end of World War I, the psychic, together with a host of other occult arts, swept America and Europe.

As with any popular fad, charlatans who smelled a dollar at the end of man's rainbow of dreams, took up mediumship and performed amazing feats to enraptured audiences. Houdini, the greatest magician—in the sleight-of-hand sense—who ever lived, knew trickery as well as any man. He became incensed at what he saw the self-styled mediums doing. He thought the whole spiritualist business was so much hogwash, but the obvious sham and crude deception practiced by the stage mediums on gullible people finally got his gall up.

At the same time, Sir Arthur Conan Doyle, creator of Sherlock Holmes, was equally energetic in his support of mediums. Doyle and Houdini had many arguments over this issue, although each respected the other's sincerity. The relationship became very complex. An unparalleled master of deception, Houdini had taken to giving public séances which were, as far as anyone could tell, absolutely authentic and real. When he was finished, he would explain to the audience just how he did it. Doyle didn't like this one bit; he angrily explained Houdini's ability to manufacture a splendid séance as a hidden gift for mediumship, which Houdini refused to accept and even ridiculed. In a letter dated 1920, Doyle wrote Houdini: "Yes, you have driven me to the occult! My reason tells me that you have this wonderful power, for there is no alternative, tho' I have no doubt that, up to a point, your strength and skill avail you."

Houdini challenged mediums again and again with enormous money offers, but no one had the courage to take on the master. He determined that his death would be the acid test of the whole medium idea.

He and his wife Beatrice arranged a code, known only to them. It was one they had used in their "mind reading" acts, and since they had guarded it like the crown jewels, they were confident that no one but them knew the cipher. Houdini agreed to do anything possible after death to get in touch with his wife, but only through this secret code. When the great stage magician finally died in 1926, Beatrice offered $10,000 to any medium who could communicate the code, which became known as the Houdini Code. Many greedy would-be spiritualists tried for the prize, but none managed to present the necessary evidence. She finally tired of sifting through the "messages" purported to come from her husband and, in 1928, withdrew the offer.

In that same year, the Reverend Arthur Ford, a Disciples of Christ minister who was aware of and immersed in his psychic abilities, was holding a trance séance in New York. In this trance, he received, through his control on the other side, a deceased French-Canadian called "Fletcher," a message purporting to come from Houdini's mother. Those attending the trance were able to verify the content of the message. They passed it on to Houdini's wife. Her interest rose. The word "forgive," supposedly coming from Houdini's mother through the trance, struck Beatrice as being an authentic message. Evidently, Houdini had waited a lifetime for this reassuring word from his mother. There were other personal items that added to the persuasiveness of the message.

Ford continued to receive messages from Houdini, through Fletcher. One night in early 1929, while Ford was in a deep trance, Fletcher, speaking through Ford, gave a message from Harry Houdini. Houdini explained the arrangements he and his wife made about the ten-word code, and wanted her to arrange a meeting with Ford. During this trance he, Houdini, would communicate the cipher. When Beatrice heard this news, she could hardly believe her ears. She came to Ford's séance with two friends.

According to Ford's autobiography, *Nothing So Strange,* Houdini revealed the code as he and his wife communicated. It was a cipher based on ten words, each representing one of the first ten letters of the alphabet. The rest of the letters were constructed by making combinations of the first ten words:

Pray A	Now D	Speak G	Be quick J
Answer B	Tell E	Quickly H	Pray-Pray K
Say C	Please F	Look I	Pray-Answer L
			etc.

Then the agreed upon message came through: ANSWER ** TELL ** PRAY ** ANSWER ** LOOK ** TELL ** ANSWER ** ANSWER ** TELL, which deciphers as BELIEVE— the word only Houdini and his wife knew about.

When the newspapermen got hold of the news, Arthur Ford became an overnight celebrity among a population seething for assurance that spiritualism was a reality. Every session had been attended by an editor of *Scientific American* and the transcript was published eventually. In the ensuing publicity, covering two continents, Beatrice was quoted as denying the story, although a letter, purporting to be in her handwriting, has been published in which she affirms everything that happened was true. As a result, this experiment, seemingly so conclusive, has too many loose ends for the outsider to come to an objective opinion. It has neither proved nor disproved communication with spirits, although it is one of the most interesting "test" cases recorded in psychical literature.

Arthur Ford, quite naturally, felt that the séance was a true communication with Houdini, although he openly admitted that there are fake mediums around.

I am not convinced that every medium is an outright fraud, nor am I convinced that spirit communication is a fact. What I do believe is that in certain mediums something authentic happens which is paranormal and deserves further investigation. The number of authentic mediums, in this sense, is small, and one should be alerted to the possibility of fraud. Not everyone who says "I am a medium, pay me" is a true psychic.

There are some quick clues to spotting fakers. Be suspicious of any physical movement or sounds during a séance. Frauds like to jazz up their performance by rocking the table, or bringing forth weird "2001: Space Odyssey" music from behind the drapes, floating "poltergeists" through the air, or having the spirits rap on the table. This sort of thing is almost always a fraud. If the séance looks like something in the movies, it is probably done the same way—by a Special Effects Department.

For instance, an enterprising medium may invite the sitters into a dimly lit room. To insure that he is being honest, he asks the people on his right and left to hold his hands and put one of their feet on his. He may explain that this transmits psychic energy or something. So far this seems clean and aboveboard, but good mediums of this stripe can slowly and imperceptably move their feet and hands so that the people on each side are holding the same hand and stepping on the same foot. This leaves him one hand and one foot free to manipulate his special effects.

Professional mediums often use a "cabinet." It may be a real cabinet, with doors, or just a curtained-off area. Behind this curtain stands the table with the instruments that the spirits will play. It is also a convenient place where the medium can effect a materialization, or conduct the rest of the highly skilled trickery that Houdini exposed to no avail.

The holding-hands-to-form-a-psychic-union bit is a clue that you are in the process of being suckered. Spirit rapping, those little knocks on the table as the departed spirits seek entrance to the séance, also reveal a hoax. In short, be suspicious of any séance that looks and acts as your imagination says a séance should.

Dedicated psychics will be the first to warn you against frauds, because getting rid of the quacks is the first major step toward uncovering whatever the truth may be about authentic communication experiences. Some authentic mediums may use these devices, and any blanket condemnation is dangerous to make—but in a field such as this, it is far better to be overly safe than credulously sorry. The current trend is toward developing one's own psychic powers. Arthur Ford, before his death in 1971, said that the day of the "professional" medium is about over.

In a séance worthy of attention, things are very simple. Expect that the medium will go into a trance state, for this seems to be a necessary condition. Communication depends upon the receptivity of the medium and trancelike states open the individual to suggestion and control from beyond. The medium insists on silence, too. Arthur Ford used a blindfold to separate himself from outside stimuli.

Communication may be established through a control, who speaks through the medium's vocal cords, although the accent may be different because the voice is that of the control and not the medium. A control is a discarnate who establishes a relationship with a medium and acts as a master of ceremonies, conveying messages from the one being contacted.

The conversation between the sitter and the discarnate (psychic term for the deceased spirit) often consists of mere trivia. The unsubstantial content of most spirit conversations makes skeptics laugh aloud. Little information filters through about the state of the future life, a topic in which mortals have a profound interest. The most common message from a departed loved one consists of such reassuring words as "Everything is all right. I am happy. I love you." A skeptic dismisses this as a canny device for creating belief by telling the bereaved sitter what he wishes to know. It makes sense though, if the discarnate is really "living" on the other side, he would reassure his loved ones left behind.

A good deal of the communication, especially at the start of the contact, involves these little items that belong to the mutual memory of the discarnate and the sitter. In a sitting with Ford, Jerome Ellison, a writer researching psychic phenomena, made contact with Fletcher, Ford's control. Fletcher said a man named Burch was interested in him. Ellison replied he had a Sunday school teacher named Burch. Then Fletcher mentioned a rabbit, but Ellison could not relate the rabbit to Mr. Burch. A year later, while visiting home, he told this incident to his mother. "You mean you don't remember? The white rabbit was an Easter present given you one year by your Sunday school teacher, Mr. Burch." Consequently, psychics point to trivia as a verification of spirit communication, because the spirit wants to identify himself in a definite way that the sitter will not question. Memories from childhood are favorite items, along with those little, intimate points that, by the time the sitter speaks with the discarnate, may have slipped his mind.

The little details supplied from the other side often become persuasive for the most skeptical. When H. Richard Neff, a skeptical clergyman who was researching prayer, went to see Arthur Ford in 1968 for a sitting, Fletcher put him in touch with eight persons, five of them being relatives of Neff. Three of the relatives were ancestors Neff had never personally known.

Later, Neff, wrote of his experience: "After the sitting was over, we admitted to each other that we had had an unusual experience. Being somewhat skeptical, we began to try to verify what Fletcher had told us. At this point, over a year later, we have investigated everything that we were told at that sitting. One piece of evidence, which involves genealogical research that we have been unable to do, remains to be confirmed. . . . Of all the evidence Fletcher gave, only three relatively minor details proved to be untrue. With the exception of the unverified genealogical evidence, everything else has proved to be accurate."[1]

An authentic séance will produce this kind of information, at least at the start. It is verifiable data; you can check its authenticity and consider the possibility of the medium knowing this information through other means. If you are convinced the data comes from an unknown source, you will come back for another try. If not, you will go home convinced spiritualism is a total fraud. But unless this kind of checkable, testable data is forthcoming, you should leave the séance right away.

Assuming for a moment that there are authentic, though paranormal, experiences involved in a true séance, does this prove that

1. H. Richard Neff, "The Church and Psychic Phenomena," *Trends,* May/ June 1970, p. 17.

the spirits are alive? Where might the information come from, if not from a discarnate? One theory offered is the super-ESP notion. The medium, using clairvoyant powers, or drawing upon unknown telepathic capacities of his sitters, taps into their unconscious pool of memory. This in itself would be a startling thing, that anyone should have such abilities. It would, however, dismiss the communication idea. The early research in ESP, as we said, indicated mediums got information from somewhere by nonsensible means, but it came to no conclusions about the source.

Another skeptical theory understands the behavior of the medium as personality disassociation, which is commonly called a "split personality." Under the influence of the trance, a medium—call her Mrs. G.—loses the control that keeps her as G–1 and psychologically takes on all the characteristics of the supposed person from beyond. In other words, Mrs. G–1, the woman who met you at the door is now Mrs. G–2, a totally different personality. Psychiatric literature records a number of these instances. Some small degree of personality disassociation is rather common in clinical instances. Most of us "normal" people have had the strange feeling once or twice that we were somebody else, that we felt entirely strange in our own skin. However, the classic form where one personality completely takes over another, such as the manifestations in a séance would require, are distinctly rare. Most psychiatrists see a lifetime of patients without observing a pure case of multiple or split personality.

At the same time, anyone who has attended the emotionally charged services in a Pentecostal church has seen people "possessed" by the "Holy Spirit." They will twitch (as some mediums do in their trances) and utter unintelligible sounds, called "speaking in tongues." I have seen individuals who, in a totally different voice from their own, would, under this kind of trance, speak understandable words claiming they were Moses, or Paul, or some other biblical worthy. This temporary form of personality disassociation—probably what really went on during the medieval demon possession scares—might explain a medium's behavior, but doesn't help much in understanding where he gets his information.

Psychical theorists with a religious bent dislike these explanations because they attack the concept of survival after death, one idea that both a spiritualist and a Christian holds dear, and which he hopes these kinds of communications are going to prove.

There is no question that reliably reported occurrences at séances are of such a nature that they stretch conventional psychological explanations to the breaking point. We have data at hand which our present conceptual framework can't handle. One explanation is simple: spirit communications are simply what they seem to be. But there may be another explanation coming forth as parapsychological research grows and develops. Dr. J. B. Rhine has not accepted the survival hypothesis and is looking for another. In the meantime, a cautious approach seems prudent, as Bishop James Pike adopted in his spiritualist investigations.

The case of the late Bishop James Pike, the flamboyant Episcopal bishop whose maverick ways never failed to excite his church, deserves a close look. More than anyone else, Bishop Pike, through books such as *The Other Side,* has given respectability to the psychic movement and helped create the flurry of interest in paranormal phenomena.

Bishop Pike's career was fascinating. Once an agnostic, he began his career as a lawyer and later, after his conversion, entered the Episcopalian priesthood. He served in parishes and did university work (Columbia University chaplain), eventually becoming the Dean of the Cathedral of St. John the Divine in New York City, a highly prestigious office. He made a name for himself by his critical attitude toward conventional church dogma, although God fascinated him. The expected role for a distinguished cleric is to preserve and defend the true faith, but Pike's restless search after truth, wherever it might lead, kept him from mouthing the homilies that went with his office. He proclaimed, for example, that the usual stuff taught in Sunday schools was thinly disguised anti-Semitism. Increasingly, he moved toward the liberal side of theology, as more and more dogmatic issues became for him open-ended questions. He associated closely with Paul Tillich, probably the greatest religious and philosophical mind of our times.

As his career developed, his home life disintegrated bit by bit.

Unsettled marriages aren't unusual for men whose basic posture to life is a quest for the most elusive of all prizes, the Truth, but distinguished clerics are supposed to have happy homes, or at least put on a good front.

The California Diocese elected him Bishop, and he moved across the country in 1958 to assume his new duties. His relationship with his wife deteriorated and he and his son, Jim, Jr., drifted apart. Finally, being an honest man, he divorced his wife, even though such a step is close to blasphemy in the Episcopal church, which frowns on divorce for anyone and is aghast when a bishop even contemplates such a move. His diocese eased him out of office, although his church did not remove his bishop's title. He endured the ordeal of a "heresy" trial on the grounds that his theology was too liberal, then moved south from his See in San Francisco to become one of the resident minds of Robert Hutchin's research group, the Center for the Study of Democratic Institutions in Santa Barbara. During this time, he began to explore new dimensions of spirituality on a more philosophical and psychical plane, because of strange events that happened to him in England. He finally announced his intention to marry his research assistant, Diane Kennedy. When the Episcopal church refused to give him an ecclesiastical wedding, he renounced his church. Still writing, still searching, James Pike made another trip to the Holy Land with his new wife, to get closer to the source of Christianity in a physical way. On this trip, while driving in the barren desert, he became lost. Diane survived, but Bishop Pike was found, after a long search, dead from exposure.

This capsule portrait gives us an image of a brilliant man, totally sincere and honest, yet one who suffered intellectual anguish, spiritual unhappiness, personal trials, and alienation within his family. With this in mind, we can go to the strange happenings in England and perhaps have some insight into how they came to change Pike's life.

After seven years as Bishop of California, his diocese arranged a sabbatical leave for him. He went for six months to study at Cambridge. At the time, he was deeply troubled about his son, Jim, Jr. Jim was using drugs such as LSD and marijuana so heavily that Pike became intensely worried. He knew he wasn't intimate with his son, and this sabbatical leave seemed like the time to get reacquainted. Jim agreed to join his father in England. Pike recalled those first days in Cambridge as the closest he and his son had ever been. Jim began to take greater interest in his studies at the British college where he enrolled, determined to quit drugs, and it looked as though it would be a beautiful and warm time.

Events now took a tragic turn. Jim, a very unhappy, restless lad, could not quit psychedelic drugs, despite his father's best efforts to help him. Jim's school work was in a mess and it looked as if he would have to return home to enroll in San Francisco State. Bishop Pike had to come back for a diocesan convention. So in February, 1966, both came back to the United States—Pike directly to San Francisco and his son to New York, to visit some friends for a couple of days. At the convention, Pike received the stunning news: Jim was dead, he shot himself in a New York hotel room at age twenty-two.

When Pike returned to Cambridge, a number of psychic events occurred in the apartment where he lived with Jim, events witnessed by his chaplain, David Barr, and his secretary. One morning all the clocks stopped at 8:19, which was the time his son probably died. Safety pins turned up around the apartment, all opened at the angle a clock's hands make at 8:19. Books and records connected with his son moved their positions and locations. Religious books and Bibles would appear opened to passages on eternal life. Once there was a commotion from the closet and when the three opened the door, they found a pile of clothing scrambled on the floor. A visitor remarked that it would be helpful if some of these events occurred when other witnesses were present. Suddenly, Jim's shaving mirror rose from the top of the bureau and drifted gently to the floor.

England has been in love with the psychic for a long time, and Anglican churchmen often devote time to studying psychic phenomena. It wasn't unusual then when the bishop of Southwark, Mervyn Stockwood, suggested that Pike visit a medium. He recommended Mrs. Ena Twigg, a matter-of-fact person who makes no pretensions about her gifts but simply accepts them. Her common-sense approach impressed Pike, who at the time was far from a committed believer in spiritualism. He agreed to a sitting and apparently, at least in his opinion, made contact with his son—at least the information given through Mrs. Twigg caused Pike to pause.

Later, Pike consulted other mediums. One was Arthur Ford, who allegedly broke the Houdini Code. In September, 1967, they appeared on Canadian television in what was a promotional effort for a book on psychic phenomena written by the religion editor of the Toronto *Star*. This interview has been shown on several TV stations and is something of a modern psychic classic. It catapulted Reverend Arthur Ford (once again) into the headlines.

Ford, blindfolded, made contact with Fletcher, and through this control, to Jim, Jr. There were a number of clues given to which Pike nodded agreement. Jim reassured his father that he need not feel guilty, that he (Jim, Jr.) had gone back on LSD and taken a bad trip.

In the course of his many sittings, Pike communicated with his friend Paul Tillich, and a number of other persons close to him in his life.

While at Cambridge, Pike, forever cautious and hesitant with his intellectual convictions, had lectured on the doubtfulness of life after death. Now he plunged himself into an intense study of psychic phenomena, confident that the medium experiences he had were honest ones, although he was not prepared to say exactly what they meant. He said again and again that psychic phenomena were new data, and that they must be taken seriously and eventually incorporated in a new hypothesis.

During one sitting with Mrs. Twigg, Jim spoke at length about conditions on the other side. It was a beautiful place. Jim spoke of God and Jesus as spiritual forces rather than personalized beings, and said that on the other side one knows true life: "I want you to know it is exciting, it's exciting. Do you know how exciting it is to come back? To be dead—but we are not the dead ones, you are the dead ones, you are the dead ones, because you are only firing on two cylinders. I want so much to tell you about a world where everybody is out to create a greater sense of love and harmony. A world in which music and color and poetry are all interwoven, making a majestic pattern. . . ."[2]

Before his own premature death, this recent doubter in eternal life wrote to those who asked if he believed (as carefully distinguished from *know*) in ongoing personal life and communication with his son, an affirmative "Yes, I do."

When one reviews Pike's life before exploring his psychic experiences, it is easy to come to an accepted conclusion: This is a classic instance of a guilt-ridden, confused father seeking reassurance that he is not responsible for the short, tragic, and painful life his son lived. On the other hand, it also emphasizes Pike's caution, devotion to truth, and the fact that he did not go to a medium believing in the psychic, or even in the traditional Christian doctrines of the afterlife. Yet, he came out a believer. You can view the whole affair as a pathetic delusion on his part, aided by a conspiracy of mediums who took advantage of his grief . . . but reading his books and learning to know his life, makes that judgment seem as unsoundly dogmatic as the assertion that his experiences "prove" communication with discarnates.

In any case, the experience of Pike is a perfect example of how people have renewed their spirituality, restored their faith in God and the spirit world—the supernatural, in other words—through psychic experiences.

This describes the motivation behind huge numbers of people who are becoming seriously interested in the psychic world. They are not interested simply in communicating with the dead, because that loses its charm after a while, unless you neurotically require continued reassurance that your loved one is all right and still thinks of you. (In England, mediums consult with departed animals, because for a Britisher, the household pet can be more important as a love object than his own wife or husband.) Psychic phenomena open doors or windows into the spiritual world, a glimpse into a sphere of reality identified with religion, which contemporary churches and our materialistic society have shut.

2. James Pike, *The Other Side* (Garden City, N. Y.: Doubleday, 1968), p. 384 (transcript of sitting with Mrs. Twigg).

These psychics stress that mediumship is merely one aspect of the total scene. The main point is that people have psychic, intuitive powers that parallel those of religious giants, and these powers are manifestations of supernatural agencies. Often, the seekers after the psychic are devout members of a denomination, but unable to find a God-experience within its framework of worship and piety.

I interviewed a woman, Mrs. Delores Sejda, who is a Roman Catholic and devotee of the modern version of the psychic movement. She is an agent for operatic singers, publicist and teacher; a college graduate, very intelligent and emotionally sensitive. Her story is fairly typical of many people I talked with.

"I have always felt that people who lead good lives can sometimes view life uncluttered. I think this is what the great mystics and saints of the church managed to do. I deliberately tried to live this kind of life, patterned, I guess, after what the nuns taught me at school. I have always felt there was an outcome to every action, that good actions bring good results and vice versa.

"From my childhood days—and I was always one of those 'mature' children—I have been aware that I could sense things and perceive deception. It didn't occur to me then that this insight was odd at all; I simply assumed everyone had it. But I knew, or felt, I could see things with less clutter and more clarity. My mind was free.

"I continued to have these intuitive psychic feelings, which I think come from God. I got my present position by following a flash of insight; there is no reason I should be working where I am except that I sensed they needed someone like me—without any foreknowledge—and I went in for an interview. They were looking for a publicist with my qualifications and asked me how I knew they needed someone, because they hadn't yet advertised the position.

"My father was a doctor, a man I consider almost saintly. I was with him when I had the experience that really changed my life.

"In 1956, our family went to the Vatican to meet Pius XII. My father was very devout in the church and knew a lot of people in the hierarchy, so we met an apostolic delegate whom my father knew, and he arranged for us to sit in the front row at the papal audience. Pius XII struck me as a very saintly man. When he passed by, I felt he could see inside my soul. He went by with his entourage giving general blessings, then he suddenly stopped and came back to my father. This is very unusual for a pope. My father was there with his rosary, and the pope asked one of his men to bring him my father's beads. He personally blessed them. Our whole family marveled at it.

"On the way home, we unfortunately booked passage on the *Andrea Doria*, which sank at sea. It was a foggy night as the ship floundered and we had lost all hope for rescue. On board were a group of seminarians returning from Rome and they offered all the Catholics a general absolution. I thought, 'O God, I'm sorry for my sins, but not so sorry that I want to die.' My father put his blessed rosary out of the window, blessing the water and praying. He turned around, looking very peaceful. He said, 'Everything will be all right.' Within one hour, the fog lifted and help arrived.

"My fiancé called me on the radio-telephone, but, you know, his voice didn't seem important, his words didn't make an impression. I knew then that only one thing counted in life—the spiritual, one's relationship with God.

"Most people who turn to psychic phenomena have had some kind of turning point experience. I felt I had to live on a new plane, to reshape my life and give it purpose.

"Psychics usually keep in the faith of their birth, but it becomes much broader. The strictures of the church cease to hamper you because you have seen a higher truth, a oneness with God, that makes these earthly things seem small and inconsequential. Truth is immutable; these other things don't matter. This gives psychics a common ground—it is the only real ecumenical thing going on because we have really transcended our spiritual rifts instead of talking about them.

"Jeane Dixon told me that the religion of the future will go back to its original simplicity—believers and nonbelievers.

"Sure a lot of people think the psychic is Lucifer's work. I know he is supposed to be very subtle and all that, but my psychic friends are basically good people—I can't believe they are instruments of evil. The psychic is a life-affirming force. It puts you in touch directly with the spiritual realm, and you realize how transitory all these earthly matters are. It gives a peace and confidence that I never knew before."

This story has psychic overtones, but otherwise it would be a classic tale of a Christian mystic.

Mrs. Sejda has communicated directly with her now deceased father. He came to her one night as she meditated before going to sleep. She had fixed her attention on an object in the room, to focus her mind and thought about her father. Presently, the distinct odor of ether came to one of her nostrils. "I thought, 'how like Dad to come to me that way,'" she told me. "I used to go with him as a child when he made his hospital rounds and we always talked about the smell of ether. He knew I would know this was him."

Her experience with her father could be called self-hypnosis. She loved her father deeply, even intensely. Naturally, she wanted the close relationship with him to continue from life into death. Her technique of meditation, suggested by Arthur Ford and used by mystics everywhere, induces a trance state, in which psychic phenomena occur. Scientifically, these happenings result from the hypnotic state; spiritually explained, they free the mind to perceive other realms. God has always communicated to men through some material means. Any religious or psychic experience must necessarily involve some mental operation or mechanism. If you look at the *how*, you stick with scientists. Religious people focus on the *what* of the experience.

Most religious mystical experiences have a trace of hypnosis in them: visions, trances, "transporting to the third heaven," and so forth. My clearest visionary experience with the reality of God came during a Tenebrae service on Maundy Thursday. In this service, worshipers recite psalm after psalm, as the sanctuary lights grow dim. After twenty minutes, I thought "What a dumb way to spend an evening. I'm bored to tears with all these psalms." After nearly an hour, the lights suddenly went out as we were invited to pray. There in the darkness, my mind flashed bright illuminations and I felt a physical presence of peace. More than at any other time in my life, I felt a prayer was truly a communication—I had come to the presence of the Holy.

Because all this happened in a church building, it can be called a religious rather than a psychic experience. It probably isn't hard to explain the dynamics. During the monotonous repetition of psalms, I was lulled into a low-grade trance while my subconscious filled with the rich religious symbolism of the Psalmist's words. When the moment for prayer came, announced in a Tenebrae service with a loud sharp noise, the flood of stored imagery rushed forth into my consciousness and I had a momentary hallucination with religious content. I know all that, but it doesn't make any difference. I know repetition, whether the "Om" of a hippie or the Rosary of a Catholic, is a technique for inducing mystical experiences. I had a trip, I enjoyed the trip. I felt a peace I had never felt before, and I liked that peace. I felt a oneness with all the world, above and below, and I delighted in that unifying vision.

It vastly oversimplifies the psychic world to say that it is wholly and solely a spiritual quest, a self-conscious effort toward spirituality. Among some religiously inclined people, it is, but there are other approaches to it.

The realm of the psychic, so weakly understood, can easily become a fearsome place to walk, a world filled with terror and the modern equivalents of the "beasties in the night." Psychic phenomena describe the broad spectrum of behaviors and manifestations we also call witchcraft and magic. The difference is one of intent—good or evil motivation of the devotee—and of style— because some modern white "witches" are sensitive and indulge in the same activities as people in the psychic movement who despise the word "witch."

A good bit of the current wave of enthusiasm for the occult in any form is a hope that it will give its adept a particular power over other people, or over destiny. These people seek to manipulate their world instead of standing in reverence before it. By definition, as we mentioned earlier, this distinction makes the difference between magic and religion.

Ghosts and other physical manifestations of the departed spirits capture our imagination, but as far as we know that is just where they exist. We all know about haunted houses. Bishop Pike recalls odd sounds in a rectory he occupied in Poughkeepsie, New York early in his ministry. Pike's consultant in England, the bishop of Southwark, wrote two articles for the London *Times* in April 1969 (reported in *Time* magazine, May 30, 1969, pp. 49–50) in which he announced he believed in ghosts. Bishop Southwark is vice-president of the Anglican-oriented, but unofficial Church's Fellowship for Psychical and Spiritual Research. He claims he communicated with the dead on five instances. He told a reporter that once "an elderly, sad looking woman" appeared at the foot of his bed. Later a spiritualist corroborated the event and traced the ghost's path through the mansion.

Gertrude Schmeidler, writing in the *Journal* of the American Society of Psychical Research, a group that tries to explore objectively these paranormal happenings, conducted a scientific investigation of a haunted house (*Journal*, April 1966). She brought sensitives to a house said by its occupants to be haunted. The family gave a full ghost report to her and then the sensitives, ignorant of the family's information, came in to explore around and try to sense the presence of the ghost and determine his character. The experiment was tightly controlled. Nine sensitives took part, using maps of the house to indicate where they felt the ghost had appeared and so forth. In some cases, the sensitives did better than chance. She concluded that "the family's reports of a ghost were confirmed at a high level of statistical significance. Beyond that, the question of what the family and the sensitives were responding to, is still open."

Telepathic and clairvoyant experiences, especially as related to premonitions, have been collected by psychical research groups for study. In spontaneous instances, as opposed to the cool atmosphere of an ESP laboratory test, the individual usually shows a high level of emotional involvement with his subject. Most clairvoyant and premonitory intuitions or dreams involve loved ones. Psychiatrists sometimes report telepathic and clairvoyant experiences between themselves and their patients, because this therapeutic relationship is charged with emotion and love-hate ambivalence. Mrs. Sejda told me of a number of her intuitions and premonitions that came to pass, often of a tragic kind.

The frequency with which clairvoyance and tragedy connect is intriguing. Miss Dixon's great prophecy attended on an assassination—in fact, assassination prophecies are very common. Edgar

Cayce, a clairvoyant prophet of renown wrote in his prophecy, *Earth Changes*, about the future of the last half of the twentieth century. (He died in 1945.) He included such choice items as parts of our coastal shores slipping into the ocean before 1998, strife "above Australia," the Great Lakes flowing into the Gulf of Mexico, and portions of Lost Atlantis rising from beneath the sea. This connection between premonition and tragedy led Dr. Edward Hitschmann to conclude that "like every form of superstition, clairvoyance is largely made up of an expectation of evil and . . . has its origin in suppressed hostile and cruel impulses."

Psychic healings, in which the sensitive can heal illness, occupy a large role in the movement. Whether one goes to a witch, or an old crone with "powers," or to a psychic lecturing in a major metropolitan church, or goes to a tent meeting at which a revivalist heals in "Jesus' holy name. Amen," the dynamics are the same. So many illnesses have psychosomatic complications that such healings are often quite real. But the powers involved aren't necessarily supernatural, because family doctors have used the same devices for years, such as prescribing a placebo, calling it a wonder drug, following which the patient suddenly improves.

Fascinating psychic phenomena involve time travel. The famous Bridie Murphy case is an example: someone reports the full details of a previous existence; such phenomena excite reincarnationists who allege that this is an instance of remembering their condition in a former life. Psychics refer to it as time travel. The work by Dunne explaining the "fourth dimension" was motivated by a desire to provide a philosophical foundation for this kind of activity. Psychologists explain these phenomena as pure instances of a disassociated or split personality. The content for the former life, according to this psychological theory, comes from reading or other inputs of information the subject received in his normal personality. Time distortion under hypnosis probably has a close connection with this kind of psychic process.

Another psychic wonder is called psychometry, which is not a separate *psi* phenomenon, but a form of clairvoyant "free association," as Edsall calls it. The sensitive or medium holds an object that belongs to someone unknown to him. He proceeds to uncover its history and facts about the owner through the object itself.

The problem is not that phenomena such as described here go on; there are well-authenticated instances of each of these kinds of *psi* activity. The real question is, what does it all mean? Psychics go off the deep end, sometimes right into an asylum, not because they explore paranormal behavior but because of the interpretation they put on it.

If you say, "All this means I have a power to destroy people and get rid of my hate," you are halfway psychotic already.

If you say, "These are *psi* processes which are a natural though little understood function of human personality," you are taking the point of view of parapsychologists.

Interpreting the meaning of these experiences as, "Basically minus behavior, the compensations of inadequate egos and unhealthy releases of repressed wishes and desire," you will be in the camp occupied by most psychiatrists.

"This means that there are supernatural powers abounding on the world scene. Each of us can participate in the spiritual realm through our psychic capabilities. The psychic shows us tangibly that life continues after death and removes our fear of dying." Such interpretation makes you feel at home with modern psychics.

Most of us, however, will probably adopt the good old cop-out called the middle-of-the-road: The facts are there, and I shall keep an open mind while I await a further hypothesis. This is essentially where investigators as different as J. B. Rhine and Bishop Pike took their stand.

One psychic phenomenon that has been reported—but by its nature is hard to verify—is the aura. Sensitives say they can see auras around people, an enveloping nimbus of light. The color and shape varies from person to person and skilled interpreters of the aura claim they can read the state of your health and morals by the condition of your aura. Eastern mystics see these auras and from this source the notion crept into a number of quasi-Eastern theosophical cults. The nimbus surrounding holy figures in early Christian art has been said to represent the aura.

My first encounter with the aura idea came while talking with LSD users. A number of them said that when they were tripping, other people seemed surrounded by a nebulous light. "It is like, well like a materialization of a personality, all the thoughts and feelings he has converted into another form, another sense, the sense of sight. You could see their thoughts. Beautiful, beautiful," as one tripper told me. LSD and other drugs, providing new mental experiences that relate to what we call psychic phenomena, have encouraged the exploration of this kind of *psi* experience. Users of heavy hallucinogens know these things can happen and try to duplicate them in real life. The peephole that LSD gives us into new dimensions of thought—if indeed that is what it does—unleashed the new search after man's hidden mental capacities.

Edgar Cayce claimed to see auras and from them he diagnosed diseases. Currently, Dr. Shafica Karagulla, a Turkish-born woman M.D., who read Cayce's writings, investigated them and turned to psychical research, is working on the aura of man. "Perhaps the human mind is developing a perceptive faculty that can quickly encompass the world of facts and move directly to perceive meaning and relationships," she wrote in 1967. That statement echoes several I have heard from LSD users, who tell me that under the drug they achieve clarity of vision, and instant communication with others, "like on thought waves only" as one young man said. Psychic theorists, such as Arthur Ford, relate the aura to man's spiritual body, as opposed to his physical body.

Whether or not this idea proves worthy of scientific interest depends on the yet unsettled prior question: Are LSD-type experiences actual human potential which is hidden in our normal state, or are they pure delusion? Those who have had good trips—either psychically, religiously, or chemically—hope it does represent true human potential. It is too beautiful, they say, to be missed.

Religions of the East and West are filled with what can be called psychic phenomena: the feats of the yoga, trances, prayer, visions, "tongues," healings through faith or prayer, blessings achieved through meditation, confidence in life after death, stigmata, sense of communication with the saints who have died—the list is endless. When they go on under religious auspices, the church tends to think they are proper, or at least tolerable. When they are labeled psychic, the church often attacks the same phenomena that appear so frequently in its own history.

In the United States, the Spiritual Frontiers Fellowship, with over 6,000 members attempts to bridge the gap between the mystical and the psychical within the recognized framework of the Christian church. It was founded by a group of clergymen and laymen, including the Reverend Arthur Ford, in 1956. They publish *Spiritual Frontiers*, a sixty-four page quarterly, a newsletter, lesson, and psychogram, and have headquarters at 800 Custer Avenue, Evanston, Illinois, 60202. Chapters meet in major cities.

I asked the Reverend William Rauscher, an Episcopal priest who serves a parish in Woodbury, New Jersey, and former President of SFF, how this group hopes to relate parapsychology, psychic research and religion.

"We are Christian in origin and emphasis," he told me. "I think the biblical idea of the gifts of the spirit is a reality and if there are implications which can be drawn from scientific pursuits for the deeper spiritual understanding of the unseen, then there should be an interpretative link with these disciplines. SFF is concerned with prayer, healing, and life after death. It is also concerned with the mystical experiences of ordinary people. It understands that there is a dividing line between the traditional mystical experience and the psychic experience, but also that they overlap. The psychic world does have its dark forces! Some people do go off on wrong paths in their co-called spiritual quests. I think this is evident in the rise of activity in witchcraft and magic. But the really fantastic surge of interest in the psychic today and the general interest in all phases of ESP does mean our work is growing in importance. The psychic factor is a stepping stone which can curse or bless! It depends on the framework within which it is perceived. We think the Christian should know about such things. All experience and study should have as its final aim a closer identity with Christ and further insight of why he did what he did.

"The study of psychic phenomena does bring into focus other realms. It does help to unite fact and faith. Religion, once called factless faith, and science, called faithless fact, find a meeting ground. In reality the unseen world is open to all of us. The direction we give our motives and the kind of experience we have as students of the subject does help to link us with the 'world of spirit.' Not meaningless occult phenomena or the dramatic, but an approach that leads to biblical style spiritual growth.

"Our Fellowship is often caricatured as only interested in mediumship. It is only one phase of the entire field. Actually, the theme of communication with the unseen world goes on at many levels. The biblical assumption is that it is happening all the time.

"For instance, we emphasize healing, not just healing of physical disease, but healing which considers man as a whole person. Jesus' ministry was a healing ministry in this comprehensive sense. True spiritual healing is the correction of the inner life. Some do have a 'gift' that produces a physical result. They are a channel. It is not the most common form of cure. All healing is not physical.

"Basically, we are attempting to create a revitalized spiritual consciousness within the church and to bring back some of the interests that gave the church life in the beginning. We feel it has strayed very far."[3]

"The paranormal experiences in Scripture," Father Rauscher explains, "come about uniquely for a holy purpose as part of the drama of our redemption to show God at work in a higher understanding which culminates in a new revelation of life after death. This is what the Resurrection is about. It is not the 'demythologize' approach of popular theology. If you remove all paranormal reference you have only wisdom and a social message. If you remove the Easter story, you do not have a church.

"The church is sadly lacking in these areas of approach. It is

3. A recent series of offerings by the Philadelphia SFF, at a large Methodist church, included these events, which give a good idea of their interests:

"Psychic Phenomena"	Marcus Bach, Ph.D., Director of the Foundation for Spiritual Understanding
"Songs and Thoughts about Teilhard de Chardin"	Sebastian Temple, a folk-style composer
"Many Realms"	George G. Ritchie, M.D., a practicing psychiatrist
"The Oneness of All Life"	Cleve Backster, a polygraph expert
"The Healing Arts"	A panel on aspects of orthodox and unorthodox healing methods, followed by a sedate healing service
"Patterns of Prophecy"	Alan Vaughan, an editor of *Psychic Magazine*
"New Frontiers of the Mind"	Robert Bradley, M.D., a pioneer in natural childbirth techniques

difficult to find articles on prayer alone in most church publications. It is difficult to find a clergyman today who speaks well on the teaching of the inner life."

I asked him if this wasn't another form of the fundamentalist cop-out, that by cultivating the soul you have a good excuse to ignore your fellowman. "Not at all," he replied. "I support social action and all help the church can give. The church gives and has given for years. But if people had more of a sense of the holiness of the church, of the universe and the world, they would be even better activists and leaders. It is interesting that people followed a Gandhi because they sensed he had an aura of personal development, a closeness to God that could be sensed. More of our religious leaders need this."

As he spoke, I thought of the flower children I have interviewed who said the same thing, in more secular terms. And I recalled the late C. S. Lewis who took to writing fantasy novels. People wondered why he did that, but his reason was simple: books like *Out of the Silent Planet* and *Perelandra* helped make the spiritual unseen world vivid and real to their readers. Lewis was a rather orthodox Christian and a noted apologist for his faith, but as a professor of medieval English literature he was close enough to the "old religion" to see that man on earth and the world of spirit can commune richly together.

There are a number of spiritualist denominations operating today. They began in the heyday of spiritualism in the late 1800s and cling to spirit communication as proof of survival after death. Sometimes, their services combine old gospel songs with a pulpit medium who brings messages from beyond to folks in the congregation. Theirs is an odd blend of the mass séance and old-time religion. They haven't grown much recently, probably because their fixation with communication ignores other parts of *psi* phenomena that interest psychic devotees. Also they aren't very intellectual in their approach and the psychic movement is trying hard to upgrade itself. In the opinion of Reverend Arthur Ford, these churches conduct frauds under the legal protection of their "religious organization" labels.

The church, as a whole, hasn't exactly jumped on the psychic bandwagon. Nor, with the notable exception of Anglican-related communions, have they given any real encouragement to the exploration of paranormal processes, even though such things are the meat and potatoes of religion. In part this is due to ignorance; churches still think of psychics in the images of charlatan mediums. In part, it is because the churches are very rationalistic and, having gotten burned once in the evolution controversy, hesitate to venture into areas where science has not sprinkled the path with holy water. And, as Reverend Rauscher observes, large parts of mainline Christianity simply feel uncomfortable with spiritual things and prefer an ethical, unemotional approach to religion.

But even church leaders who place the spiritual values first, who support prayer and pious activity, denounce the psychic. Why all this hostility? There are a number of reasons for this.

First, literal, fundamentalistic interpreters of the Bible stand on the Levitical admonition "Do not consult mediums." That settles the issue. The whole psychic business is the Devil's creation.

Second, the Christocentricity of most churches is grounded in history. The unique Christ-event happened once and for all. He redeemed man from his sin and offers the only path to God, through his redemptive act. This doesn't allow room for the mystical Christ or evolving spirituality (spiritual evolution of man) that underlies the psychic approach to religion. In their zeal to glorify God, the traditional denominations tend to put down human nature and human spiritual capacity.

Third, if everyone can directly encounter God, then religion becomes very untidy and disorganized and the church—as keeper of the means of grace—loses its importance.

Fourth, there is the matter of revelation. Orthodox faith asserts the finality of the scriptural revelation. In the Catholic wing, tradition can, within limits, supplement this revelation. But if God is to speak to his people, he will do so through the church, which in practice means the deliberative assemblies of the institution. Private visions are always unofficial. Further, orthodox churchmen point to psychic revelation and ask, "So what's new?" The religious value of psychic experience however is not so much in finding "new" truth, but in having an experiential affirmation of known truth, so that it becomes a real, dynamic part of their lives. Life after death is surely not news to Christianity but the conviction that life sur-

117

vives comes to many devout church people through psychic experiences rather than the church's teaching on the subject.

Fifth, organized religion rightly rejects any experience based solely on feelings. Despite its high emotional nature, believers eventually need a rationale for their feelings. Psychics tend to be emotional people who live off their feelings. They build a faith around experiences. Right now, the movement is beginning to develop an underlying "theology." Groups such as SFF hope to shape that theology in the direction of the Christian tradition. Churches should recognize this trend toward a developing theology in psychic religious experience and, through sympathetic relationships to the movement, help guide it toward Christ mysticism.

Sixth, there is the problem of relating the picture of survival after death given by the psychics to the traditional church doctrines. As Jim Pike, Jr. reported, the discarnates are now "alive" and functioning in a beautiful place. Protestant doctrine leans toward the sleep theory, that the dead sleep until the final resurrection of the dead. Rejecting immortality as such, this doctrine teaches that eternal life is a gift of God, obtaining through specific divine action ("the resurrection of the dead" in the Apostles' Creed). These theologians argue that the soul is not separate from the body, that man does not have a spiritual entity within his material form that continues life hereafter. Catholic dogma teaches intermediary states, such as purgatory and limbo, and none of the psychic reports from the other side verify this. While the church firmly endorses the basic notion of survival after death, it cannot agree with the psychic interpretation of it. Many psychics told me their experiences with the beyond have erased their fear of death completely, something their churches, despite their best efforts, never accomplished.

Orthodox Christianity, as traditionally interpreted, probably can't make room for the psychic under that label. It can, however, offer from its rich treasury of faith a means—and a tangible methodology—of meditation and communion on an immediate, personal basis, with God. It can affirm with Paul, "O grave where is thy victory? O death, where is thy sting?" Unless the church recovers the mysticism which it has usually hidden under its institutional rug, it will lose contact with vast numbers of people who are searching for spiritual meaning. ℗

Magic and Religion
in the Bible

One piece of ancient literature with which most of us are familiar is the Bible. From its pages both Judaism and Christianity derive their inspiration. The biblical materials went into written form from roughly 1000 B.C. to A.D. 100, but underneath the existing strata of story and legend, we have the shadowy presence of ideas that go back even further.

In the Old Testament especially, we can expect to find traces of magic and other occult approaches to the world. We do, but not in a pure form. The biblical tradition is adamant against the profusion of occult that enveloped their tiny Israelite state. While bits and pieces of magic entered into their religious life, the highest religious tradition of Israel never felt comfortable with them. Under the growing influence of a conception of the all-powerful Yahweh, in whom one found his sole hope, the basically polytheistic rites of surrounding cultures became anathema to the Jews.

At the same time, again particularly in the Old Testament, the biblical writings reveal a fundamental posture among the Israelites that dampened the separation between the spiritual—represented by an increasingly majestic and transcendental ethical Yahweh—and the man in the world . . . a posture that consists essentially of a profound sense of unity between men and the created world.

This intimate relationship is tenderly and simply narrated in the earliest Creation story, the J tradition beginning with Genesis 2:4 ff. "So God formed out of the ground all the wild animals and all the birds of heaven. He brought them to the man to see what he would call them, and whatever the man called each living creature, that was its name" (Genesis 2:19). Not only could man name the animals, give them an identity in relationship to him, but he also shared their source of origin. Like the animals, God made man from the ground (Genesis 2:7). In Hebrew, the word translated as man in the Genesis stories is *adam* and the word for ground, or the earth from which he came, is etymologically related, *adamah*. Man and Creation are thus shown to be in an intimate and harmonious relationship, and each participate equally in the activity of God.

This mystical union between man and his world runs through all the ancient fertility cults. It is a dominant theme in original religion. The second Creation saga, written from the later P tradition, appears in Genesis 1. There, God "created man in his own image; in the image of God he created him . . ." (Genesis 1:27). In the very few centuries separating these two traditions, the nature. relatedness of man has diluted and now he and the transcendent God are connected directly through the act of Creation without any intermediaries from the stuff of creation. The Holy Yahweh begins his triumph, even as the civilization of Israel moves from the simple pastoral-agricultural life of Genesis 2 toward the more civilized beginnings of a commercial society that liked the Genesis 1 story better. The mood of the Scriptures rapidly reflects this isolation of man by its developing insistence that man shall have no idols, or false gods. Man is stripped naked before the Holy One of Israel, all his props removed, all his tangible connections with the divine—the "holy" things that one can see and touch and feel and know that one is tactilely and experimentally absorbing the unseen spiritual realm. They are condemned as interferences with his "spiritual life." During this same period, the primitive Israelite religion moved from henotheism—the toleration of other gods while holding Yahweh supreme—toward a complete, absolute, no-nonsense monotheism. The focal point of religion moves from man and his needs, dreams, and aspirations, to God and his needs, dreams, and aspirations for man; from egocentricity to theocentricity.

During the long history of Israelite religion, elements of occult practices continued and they are frankly recorded in the historical documents of that religion. Sometimes, the occult practices receive merciless condemnation, and other times they slip into the accepted faith unnoticed. This ambivalence indicates that while the Israelite faith had a powerful transcendent thrust, the people among whom it worked were close enough to the old Genesis 2 sense of oneness of Creation and man to appreciate a number of practices rational man later decried as magic, divination, and the occult.

The ankh derives its name from the Egyptian word for life, prosperity. This cross and loop symbol is a sacred emblem for life, but has no relation to the cross symbol used in the Christian tradition.

In its earliest stages, magic and ritual in Israel are too closely intertwined to unravel the traditions.

We read about taboos and spells, such as in Judges 5:23–24:

> A curse on Meroz, said the angel of the LORD;
> a curse, a curse on its inhabitants,
> because they brought no help to the LORD.

The people also used holy water to cleanse someone who had touched the dead. Made of water, the ashes from the sin-offering, and marjoram, this magical potion was sprinkled over the unclean person according to a specific ritual (Numbers 19:14 ff.) that reads like the instruction in medieval grimoires. The institution of the so-called scapegoat offering, Leviticus 16:2 ff., also reflects magical practices. Aaron, the priest, was to cast lots (divination) over the two goats, choosing one for the Lord and the other for Azazel, the wilderness demon. The latter goat wasn't sacrificed on the altar but rather loaded with the sins of the people and driven away "into the wilderness" to a precipice, over which it would fall and somehow rid the Israelite society and cultus of influences of dark power. Blood sprinkling and sacrifices to invite Yahweh's presence among the people are only a few more of the magical elements in Israelite religion. To this list, we can add the holy places, such as Shechem, which Joshua chose to enhance the authority of his covenant renewal ceremony, and Shiloh, where the ark once rested and Samuel saw the Lord (1 Samuel 3). The bells which Aaron put on his priestly robes so that "the sound of it shall be heard when he enters the Holy Place before the LORD and when he comes out; and so he shall not die" (Exodus 28:35) represent more magical elements.

Dreams are frequent means of divination in the Bible, as they were throughout the ancient world. In the Joseph cycle, we have Joseph bringing a dream suggestive of his future glory to his brothers and father for interpretation. They obviously accept the fact that the dream can be prophetically meaningful, although they don't like the message: that Joseph will one day have a position of great authority (Genesis 37:5–11). Later on, in Egypt, when Joseph was in jail on a trumped-up rape charge, the Pharaoh's chief butler and baker, also imprisoned, had dreams which Joseph neatly divined. "Does not interpretation belong to God?" he assured them as he invited them to reveal their dreams to him (Genesis 40:8). The Pharaoh had heard of Joseph's ability and asked him to interpret a dream. " 'I have had a dream, and no one can interpret it to me. I have heard it said that you can understand and interpret dreams.' Joseph answered, 'Not I, but God, will answer for Pharaoh's welfare' " (Genesis 41:15). Already the Israelite faith, while engaging in behavior suggestive of magic, shifted the focus from the magician's power to God, the Almighty One.

Even though the late story of Daniel, written at a time when Greek influence pervaded the Middle East (about the second century B.C.), features Daniel as a successful dream interpreter, the history of biblical prophets is that they soft-pedaled the dream idea and relied more on heavenly visions—what we might call intuitive prophecy.

Amos had a vision of locusts (Amos 7:4–6), and a plumb line (Amos 7:7 ff.); Hosea saw Israel's coming glory (Hosea 2:14–23); First Isaiah received his call to prophesy in a vision (Isaiah 6:1–11); Jeremiah's visions of an almond in early bloom and a cauldron, tilted to the north and on fire, receive from God a political interpretation reminiscent of intuitive prophecies down to the present day (Jeremiah 1:11–19).

The visions of these later prophets, including the unbelievably wild images of Ezekiel's wheels (which some have even interpreted as flying saucers!), are rather modest compared with the ecstatic utterances of such ancient oracles as the Delphic women. Mostly, the prophets gave their messages in a sane, normal, conscious state of mind, although the original source of their insight may have come through a paranormal, psychic vision into the heavenly councils. They railed loudly against false prophets. It has always been hard to distinguish true from false prophecy, and the gift of discernment is prominently absent from human affairs. The twenty-third chapter of Jeremiah gives us the most complete denunciation of false prophets and with it a clue to discernment.

I have heard what the prophets say, the prophets who speak lies in my name and cry, 'I have had a dream, a dream!' How long will it be till they change their tune, these prophets who prophesy lies and give voice to their own inventions? By these dreams which they tell one another these men think they will make my people forget my name, as their fathers forgot my name for the name of Baal. If a prophet has a dream, let him tell his dream; if he has my word, let him speak my word in truth. What has chaff to do with grain? says the LORD. Do not my words scorch like fire? says the LORD. Are they not like a hammer that splinters rock? I am against the prophets, says the LORD, who steal my words from one another for their own use. I am against the prophets, says the LORD, who concoct words of their own and then say 'This is his very word.' I am against the prophets, says the LORD, who dream lies and retail them, misleading my people with wild and reckless falsehoods. It was not I who sent them or commissioned them, and they will do this people no good. This is the very word of the LORD (Jeremiah 23:25–32).

Jeremiah lived about 600 B.C., a century after Isaiah, during the capture and destruction of Jerusalem. The later prophets had fought long battles with the "court prophets" who told the kings what they wished to hear ("yes-men") and blinded their royal patrons to the intensely dangerous political difficulties that beset the small Israelite nations. The prophet's key to discernment was simple: if it is what you want to hear, if it tickles your fancy, it is false prophecy; if it sears you, shakes you up, rocks your comfortable boat, it is the true word of the Lord. By this time, the word prophet, biblically speaking, comes to mean a "forth-teller" or "truth-speaker on behalf of God" rather than a diviner of omens, foreteller of the future, or a trance speaker. Even though they often cast their oracles in terms of a direct message from On High, the data sources for their advice appear quite surely to come from sensitive, moral insights into the complexities of the existing political and ethical situation.

This is a long way from the time when Elijah took on the prophets of Baal who lived on Mt. Carmel in a duel of magic and wonder-working to see which had their finger on the most powerful god—power to work wonders being the *sine qua non* of an authentic divinity. The Elijah-Elisha cycle contains a number of occult elements, including passing on a power-giving mantle from Elijah to his apprentice Elisha, healing people through personal rituals, and other behaviors suggestive of magic. However, even at this time, Israelite history distinguishes between God's activity—even though it looks like what we would call magic—and similar behaviors coming from another source. Jehu could denounce Jezebel, the mother of the king no less, right to her royal son's face: "Do you call it peace while your mother Jezebel keeps up her obscene idol-worship and monstrous sorceries?" (2 Kings 9:23). Elisha had already denounced Jezebel, a follower of Baal since she was the daughter of the king of Tyre, and prophesied her horrible death (2 Kings 9:10). Thus ended a long feud between Jezebel—representing the power of Baal—who instigated the original confrontation between Elijah and the Mt. Carmel wonder men, and Elijah and Elisha. The activities engaged in by both sides of this struggle seem quite alike to the ordinary reader; the difference, of course, is whose magic are you offering, Baal's or Yahweh's? By the time of the eighth-century prophets, the distinction between true and false prophets took on a more ethical quality.

Besides dreams, Israel pursued other forms of divination. Belomancy, or the use of arrows for advice, provided the mortally ill Elisha with the word of victory sought by his client, King Jehoash. But the king, who had to do the ritualistic procedures himself because Elisha lay on his deathbed, didn't follow the ritual properly and thus could only be sure of a partial victory over the enemy, Aram (2 Kings 13:14–19). Even in death, though, Elisha retained the magical powers Elijah gave to him. When some people unknowingly threw a body into his grave, after a Moabite guerrilla raid, the deceased touched the prophet's bones and "the man came to life and rose to his feet" (2 Kings 13:21).

Divination by casting lots was a favorite Israelite technique. The mysterious Urim and Thummim (Exodus 28:30) were probably pebbles carried by the priest to divine issues, a kind of holy dice. The land given to each of the twelve tribes when they moved into the Promised Land was determined by casting lots (Numbers 26:55). Our word "allotted" comes from the process of divination and selection by lots.

Magic symbols, such as the staff, appear in the Bible. Once Moses cast a staff on the ground and it became a snake and God used this weird transformation to convince Moses of his presence (Exodus 4:2–4). The symbol appears later in the same transformation, only this time it is used to convince Pharaoh that God is real (Exodus 7:9). Finally, the bronze serpent version of the symbol, widely honored in the ancient East, becomes a healing symbol for snake bites, from which Israelites could be cured if they gazed upon the brazen serpent (Numbers 21:8 ff.). The symbols go from a magical guarantee of power to the higher role of healing. (The caduceus of the Greek Aesculapius, used as the symbol for the medical profession, is rooted in this brazen healing-serpent tradition.)

There is one well-known instance of necromancy in the Bible, the incident when King Saul consulted the so-called Witch of Endor (1 Samuel 28:3–25). Consulting departed spirits represented, for Israel, one of the grossest reversions to occult idolatry. Very early in their history, they wrote laws against the practice: "I (God) will set my face against the man who wantonly resorts to ghosts and spirits, and I will cut that person off from his people. Hallow yourselves and be holy, because I the LORD your God am holy. You shall keep my rules and obey them: I am the LORD who hallows you" (Leviticus 20:6–8). This injunction seems to speak against the idea of finding holiness, or separation of man to divine service, through encounters with departed spirits. The Israelite faith in the afterlife differed considerably from the modern Christian version. They didn't think much about what befell man after death; he went to a shadowy place called Sheol, or The Pit. Judaism, today, less vigorously pursues the blessings of eternal life than Christianity. Judaism, historically, has concentrated attention on this life. Their seemingly worldly view is consistent with Hebrew biblical psychology.

Prior to the fourth century B.C., when the conquests of Alexander brougth the Greek idea of separate body and spirit to the Jews, they thought of man as a totality, a unity of body and soul, material and spirit. Their word *ruach* means physical breath as well as what we would call spiritual soul. It was the life-animating force, breathed into man by God at creation (Genesis 2:7). It was "the breath of life." Consequently, the Israelite—when he thought as an Israelite without influences from other cultures—couldn't conceive of a spiritualized existence beyond earthly life. From an ethical point of view, this attitude had tremendous implications. It means that the task of religion is not to minister to something called a soul, but to bring the whole of man into relationship with God. That implies tangible ministries to his worldly state—food, justice, good treatment, equality, etc. This view permitted the Jews to give a profound ethical meaning to religion.

Nevertheless, Saul, in a state of desperation, called upon the medium at Endor, even though he himself had made wizardry illegal—a point the good medium ironically mentions (vv. 2 and

9). Saul came to her in disguise, but she discovered who he really was. He was beset by worries over the impending Philistine threat. The medium conjured up Samuel, the dead prophet. Samuel gave Saul a good ethical tongue-lashing for not obeying the Lord, and said that as a result the Philistines would win. Saul, all day without food and racked with anxiety, passed out at the news and the medium, in an act of great compassion, took Saul to her home. She killed a calf for meat and baked him some cakes. Even though this story is cast in the typical conjuring-up-the-dead-to-foretell-the-future form, the content of Samuel's message was no different from that of the living prophets in that day. In other words, Saul gained no advice or straw of hope from this experience that he did not already have at hand.

The story reflects two interesting points. First, the medium, like modern practitioners, did not identify whatever it was she conjured. Saul did that. She only said she saw a ghostly form coming from the earth, an old man wrapped in a cloak. It is Saul who decided this vision was truly Samuel. Second, Samuel is said to ask Saul, "Why have you disturbed me and brought me up?" Rather than enjoying a blissful afterlife which he is anxious to talk about, Samuel has been disturbed from sleep, as it were. The place of Sheol was thought of as an eternal bedroom; since the notion of nonexistence was too hard for the ancient Jews to handle, they came as close as they could to it by equating death with sleep.

The long history of establishing the authority of one God had a political side: the process of establishing one nation. Occult and magic practices became identified with local shrines and foreign influences. When King David began to consolidate Israelite worship about a central shrine (about 1000 B.C.) the prophets followed his lead by denouncing the occult practices associated with scattered religious centers. In their fierce nationalism, the later prophets also condemned the magical practices that came to Israel through their commercial and political contacts with other nations. The weakening of the national will under Solomon was, in the prophetic view, the result of his flirting with other gods, brought to his palace by the foreign beauties with whom he liked to flirt. The fascination with occult practices that were a part of outside cults diverted Israel's leaders from the path of justice and right, to which God had called his people.

By the time Second Isaiah wrote, (after the Exile) the prophetic voices in Israel were adamant about the occult:

> I am the LORD, there is no other.
> I do not speak in secret, in realms of darkness, . . .
> I the LORD speak what is right, declare what is just . . .
> (Isaiah 45:19, 20).
> Persist in your spells and your monstrous sorceries,
> maybe you can get help from them,
> maybe you will yet inspire awe.
> But no! in spite of your many wiles you are powerless.
> Let your astrologers, your star-gazers
> who foretell your future month by month,
> persist, and save you!
> But look, they are gone like chaff;
> fire burns them up; . . .
> So much for your magicians
> with whom you have trafficked all your life:
> they have stumbled off, each his own way,
> and there is no one to save you
> (Isaiah 47:12–15).

We have seen that Israelite religion, born in the cradle of the occult, adopted some magical forms in the beginning. Later, some of these were turned to religious purposes. Over a period of centuries, often fighting against great odds, the concept of one God, whose will is justice, began to predominate, at least among the best thinkers. From fertility cult to transcendent God is a long road, yet Israel managed to travel it without being afflicted with the sense of alienation from the spiritual world that plagues modern man. They still kept the emotional feeling that God and his people were united together in an intimate fellowship.

Two ideas helped this healthy adjustment to an ethical God. First, the central idea of the covenant. God had made certain agreements with his people, pacts or treaties in which he agreed to be with them and they agreed to pursue his will. The Sinai

Covenant is the best known of these agreements. Periodically, as we read in Joshua 24, the people would gather in a worshipful assembly for the purpose of renewing their commitment to the covenant. Intellectually, the covenant idea provided a rationale for God's intimate relationship with his people. Tangibly, the people had symbols of the covenant, in the ark and the periodic assemblies, which gave them something of God's that they could touch and participate in. Through these devices, Israel managed to satisfy that need in man we call the "mystical encounter with God." In our day, this encounter often seems at odds with ethical religion, but Israel more or less successfully managed to hold the two together in these early times.

Second, the Israelites did not accept the idea of individuality which we feel today. Our modern frustration with alienation, a sense of being separated and cut off from the Ground of Being, the Ultimate Source, results largely from our lack of corporate identity. Our individualism has degenerated to a concept of the single man alone against his fellows and his God. Traditional expressions of Christianity tend to reinforce this alienation by placing God afar, from whence he calls upon man for right living and correct decisions, but leaves hapless man alone in his chamber of crisis, while holding him accountable for his actions.

Professor H. Wheeler Robinson spoke of the "corporate personality" in ancient Israel. By this he meant a bond that united individuals into one personality, in which each person shared the corporate mind. The past-present-future of an individual man was in his mental thought processes identical with the history of his people. When Hosea projected his own life experiences onto the life of Israel, it was not his massive ego that led him to think his private affairs with the whore Gomer had such general application, but his deep sense of identity with his people. The prophets who allegedly foresaw and predicted future events in Israel's life were not consciously predicting the future as such, but simply made little or no distinction between the present and the future because the history of their people was made of one piece of cloth. Westerners can't grasp this, so we tend to read the "prophecies" of Isaiah, for example, as foretelling the coming of the Messiah, or else relating to the situation of the writer's own time. Actually, Isaiah was probably speaking of the corporate future of his people which has at once a present and a future side, and an individual and corporate expression.

This is a basically tribal way of thinking, and it is among the tribal-oriented people that we often discover communications and experiences that we call occult. Visitors to Africa seem amazed at how people within a tribe know of their presence without even so much as a sound of drums to communicate from village to village. Visiting in Indonesia, I spoke with a Western professor on the Theological Faculty at Nommensen University in Sumatra. He told me how a Batak man can perceive that he is going to die. He will announce his imminent departure, gather his family for the blessings required by his *adat* or customary law, then expire. "I used to think the Old Testament was heavy on myth," he told me. "But here you live in the midst of that kind of world." Of course it is; both the Old Testament world and the Batak world are tribal lives and we in the individualized Western mold can't appreciate them.

Among Bataks, the tribal bond is called *halakita*. A rough equivalent of this among American blacks is the expression "soul brother" which has a content and depth a white man cannot grasp.

The bond of unity with God, found by Israel in the covenant, and the unification of people, which they had in the corporate tribal life through which God spoke to the people as a whole rather than to a collection of individuals, are two missing links in our Western world—and many who pursue the occult are actually searching in the buried strata of man's religious history to find them.

When Greek ideas flowed into Israel, the covenant and corporate foundations eroded and the beautiful house rattled on sand. Greek individualism, when attached to a prophetic tradition that had become increasingly individualized, shook the Israelites loose from their togetherness with each other and their oneness with God. New means of relating man and God filtered into their life from Greek and other sources. From this period we get the idea of angels, as intermediaries between God and man—quite unnecessary in the old days—and the evolving of a complex system of the afterlife. Instead of being simply "good" because God made it, the world of creation and man's own physical body became a prison from which his pure spirit must seek release. The Greeks had a number of systems for purifying the soul and gaining its release from the fetters of corporal existence. We call these systems "mystery religions."

A mystery religion is a system of revealing the secrets of God to man. "Mystery" is used in both the Old and New Testaments. Scholars once attributed the mystery concept entirely to Greek influences. There is no doubt that the word mystery—indicating God has secrets which through wisdom, faith or some psychic process man can unravel and be illuminated—appears in the late Old Testament writings. Daniel 2 is the major reference in the Protestant canon, with the Apocrypha and Pseudepigrapha (some of which are canonical in Roman Catholicism) and the Qumran writings which are also full of the concept. However, in an excellent study, Raymond E. Brown, S.S., a Roman Catholic biblical scholar, carefully traces this concept to Semitic origins. If he is correct, Israelite religion, even in the time of the major prophets, honored direct participation in God's "mysteries" as a source of revelation. This view emphasizes the point that the finest strain of Israelite religious thought allowed room for nonrational, psychical experience. See Father Brown's articles in *The Semitic Background of the Term "Mystery" in the New Testament* (Facet Books, Biblical Series 21 [Philadelphia: Fortress Press, 1968]).

At this point, we arrive at the time the New Testament was written.

The Gospels record a number of psychic phenomena (or divine visions and powers, or hallucinations, as you prefer). The birth of Jesus is announced in a dream to Joseph (Matthew 1:20). Jesus performs many healing miracles, sometimes exorcising demons (Matthew 8:16), although he declared definitely that his power was not from Satan (Matthew 12:25 ff.). His method did not stress the action involved in healing, but emphasized the faith of the cured one: "Your faith has made you well." While preparing for his ministry by going out into the wilderness, Jesus is beset with visions of satanic temptation (Mark 1:12–13 and parallels).

At one turning point in his ministry, Jesus went up on a mountain with his most intimate disciples and was transfigured: "his clothes became dazzling white, with a whiteness no bleacher on earth could equal. They saw Elijah appear, and Moses with him, and there they were, conversing with Jesus" (Mark 9:3–4). Psychics point to this as a verification for *psi* phenomena. Bible scholars, who don't like this sort of thing, dismiss the event as a legend added later, or as an example of primitive credulity by the gospel writer. Others interpret it theologically, in terms of the developing picture of Jesus' ministry, while still others—who reject the occult vigorously—assert that it really happened, but only then, on that mountain, for God's special purposes and it cannot be readily duplicated. A psychologist might say the vision was real enough to the participants, but arose from their own minds.

One psychic-like experience which the Gospels record is hard to dismiss because, theologically, it is central to Christian doctrine: the Resurrection of Christ. Most biblical scholars give greatest authority to Mark's account, which in the best manuscripts ends at 16:8 and does not record any post-Resurrection appearances of Jesus. However, the last verses of Mark, as printed in most Bibles, do record one such appearance, and the other three gospel writers also include them.

In Matthew, the risen Christ appears suddenly upon the path trod by the two Marys (Matthew 28:8–10). In Luke, he appears on the road to Emmaus (Luke 24:13 ff.) and even joins his fellows for a meal, at which time they suddenly recognize who it really is who sits at their table, and then Jesus vanishes. John records the famous doubting Thomas story, in which Jesus appears, from nowhere, in a locked room and is able to show the disciples, and on his second visit Thomas, the marks of his hands (John 20:19–25). Jesus seems to behave as an apparition, or a ghost, might be expected to do.

However, except for the visit to Thomas, the Gospels do not

132

record a postmortem visitation only for the purpose of assuring the disciples that he did, really and truly, rise from the dead. His conversations with the disciples revolve around their responsibilities and reinforce the charge he had laid upon them during his lifetime. In other words, the stories of his appearances have a point that goes far beyond merely trying to emphasize that life goes on beyond the grave.

Paranormal phenomena in the ministry of Jesus certainly exist on record, whether modern Christians feel comfortable with them or not. Yet, such paranormal occurrences have been part of religion since the beginning, until our rationalism stripped them away. Now leading theologians find no difficulty in proclaiming that all these unexplainable events are simply myths and hallucinations, thus making Jesus a purely ethical and social prophet. Believers accept this with remarkably little protest. Or at least some do—because there is a strong desire among others, as reflected in the occult revival, to restore the paranormal to religious respectability.

Certainly when Matthew recorded the coming of astrologers (Magi, or Persian magicians) to honor the baby Jesus, guided by a "star," he did not feel any urge to demythologize the event; quite the contrary, he was anxious to embellish the birth, a paranormal event without a doubt, in the most "occult" terms possible.

As the rest of the New Testament unfolds, we do not find that the apostles and dissiples avoid, like a disease, any mention of paranormal events. They healed people without physical means. On Pentecost, they spoke with a gift of tongues, suddenly becoming multilingual. The apostles healed by the laying on of hands and it is recorded that "through Paul God worked singular miracles: when handkerchiefs and scarves which had been in contact with his skin were carried to the sick, they were rid of their diseases and the evil spirits came out of them" (Acts 19:11–12).

The apostles did not simply perform magic; that is clear even to Luke who records their work. There was a profound difference between magicians and the apostles. "But some strolling Jewish exorcists tried their hand at using the name of the Lord Jesus on those possessed by evil spirits; they would say, 'I adjure you by

Jesus whom Paul proclaims.' There were seven sons of Sceva, a Jewish chief priest, who were using this method, when the evil spirit answered back and said, 'Jesus I acknowledge, and I know about Paul, but who are you?' And the man with the evil spirit flew at them, overpowered them all, and handled them with such violence that they ran out of the house stripped and battered. This became known to everybody in Ephesus, whether Jew or Gentile; they were all awestruck, and the name of the Lord Jesus gained in honour. Moreover many of those who had become believers came and openly confessed that they had been using magical spells. And a good many of those who formerly practised magic collected their books and burnt them publicly" (Acts 19:13–19).

This and other passages indicate that, in the minds of the apostles, their wonders were far different form the usual magic, even if the story reads like any other use of a magic name. Their powers came from God through Jesus and were totally unique. However, they shared one thing in common with the people of their day, an idea incorporated in the doctrine of the Incarnation: God, the supernatural divine power, can manifest himself in human life. And when God does so, he gives gifts and powers to people which are paranormal in their effect. The supernatural world enters into and alters the natural world. By theological definition, at least, this is quite different from magic, but it looks like much the same sort of thing. People wanting this window into the supernatural don't always make the delicate distinction between what comes from God and what is from nothing, the distinction so dear to theologians, because their attention is focused on the action, the paranormal experience itself. Unless one wishes to toss out completely all paranormal, psychic and magical manifestations in the documents of the Christian faith, he must find some creative way to affirm the interaction of God's realm and man's realm that avoids going off the deep end that swallows up so many occultists.

Paul, after all, came to Christian conviction following a vision on the Damascus road. So we can expect that he would not be surprised if God operated in non-normal ways. He wrote to the Corinthians that by the Spirit of God they would have certain gifts (1 Corinthians 12:4–13):

There are varieties of gifts, but the same Spirit. There are varieties of service, but the same Lord. There are many forms of work, but all of them, in all men, are the work of the same God. In each of us the Spirit is manifested in one particular way, for some useful purpose. One man, through the Spirit, has the gift of wise speech, while another, by the power of the same Spirit, can put the deepest knowledge into words. Another, by the same Spirit, is granted faith; another, by the one Spirit, gifts of healing, and another miraculous powers; another has the gift of prophecy, and another the ability to distinguish true spirits from false; yet another has the gift of ecstatic utterance of different kinds, and another the ability to interpret it. But all these gifts are the work of one and the same Spirit, distributing them separately to each individual at will.

Paul can put logical discourse and learning (reason) in the same bag with paranormal events such as healing and utterances, and call both the work of one Spirit. Hard as this is for the modern mind to grasp, Paul did it on the basis of one criterion: whatever serves a useful purpose. He knew the excesses to which the psychic and magical could go—this very passage was written to counsel the Corinthians who were going off the beam with their addiction to *glossalalia* or tongues, which has recently cropped up in Presbyterian, Lutheran, Episcopal circles far from the evangelistic pentecostal sawdust trails—but he hesitated to toss the baby out with the bathwater. He recognized the role of the paranormal in religious experience and the useful purpose it could serve. Rather than totally denounce these manifestations, he hoped to bring them into a semblance of unity and purpose by focusing them on Christ.

For much the same reason, Paul spoke of Christ mysticism, the union of man with the risen Lord in his Resurrection as well as his death. This image looks like a steal from Greek mystery religion, which promised salvation by union with a dead and risen God, and so interpreters a few years ago spoke about it. But Paul did not steal the idea directly; it rather grew out of his conception of the unity in Christ of the material and spiritual world. The concept has Semitic roots. Thus, the Lord's body could appear in the physical Eucharistic symbols of bread and wine; thus, Christ could be experientially alive in the believer's life; thus, the whole church —the people of God—is united in Christ and in close communion with each other.

This idea can sound like an occult cult. For instance,

The Great Illuminator rescued us from the domain of darkness and brought us to the Light of Truth, in which state our release is secured and we are cleansed of all evil. The Great Illuminator is the unity of all things visible and also the visible orders of thrones and powers. He exists in everything, and all things come to their focal point in the brightness of the Illuminator's resplendent brightness.

That may read like a passage from some occult book with a theosophical slant, but it is a rewrite—dropping the words God and Christ—of Colossians 1:13–20. Check the original, which says that all things begin and end and are brought together in the cosmic Christ, the focus of and omega-point for all creation.

Such a unifying vision that bridges the distance between alienated man and his world is what motivates many people to explore the occult. Paul claims it can be found in Christ and him alone.

If Paul is right, then the Church has plenty of theological resources by which to develop a neo-mysticism that embraces the normal ethical and paranormal spiritual experiences of man.

While the Bible is filled with occult behaviors and actions, and loaded with paranormal experiences, it keeps a foot on the ground by its strong insistence that spirituality is developed through serving one's fellowman. Paul writes in a mystical vein, as does John. James, on the contrary is matter-of-fact: True religion consists of helping widows and orphans in their distress (James 1:26–27). Jesus, while doing pananormal spiritual acts, spent most of his ministry giving similar advice: Love God and love your neighbor. Yet a complete religious experience for man requires both sides of the coin, and the biblical evidence at hand suggests that there is nothing unscriptural about restoring some of the experiential, subjective aspects to the Christian life.

Even though the biblical religion is hundreds of miles from the Island of the Occult, it can satisfy the fullness of man's religious needs, even those sought in the occult. The Old Testament notion of the unity of soul and body, for example, gives a picture of a unified human nature. Paul, though he used some language suggestive of a spirit-body dichotomy, never went as far with it as the Greeks did and while he pummeled his mortal flesh and fought fleshy desires, he never called the body evil. The New Testament is more otherworldly, pointing more to future rewards than does the Old Testament, but even it holds to the worth of human life as it is lived and the ability of God to penetrate and use normal human existence.

The covenant idea, taken into the New Testament as a relationship of the corporate body of believers with the risen Christ, provides an equally strong foundation for the unity of persons with persons.

We have come too far down the road of rationalism, science and individualism ever to recover the alleged purity of early man. Nor will we be able to turn back to recapture the life-styles reflected in the Bible. Attempts to restore so-called pure Christianity have failed. We must accept where we are; there is no going home, because home isn't there anymore. At the same time, the church need not close off the room that holds the treasures of spirituality and mysticism because there is ample warrant in the Scriptures for a religious life of wholeness and emotional experience, along with a powerful ethical imperative. Religion, for whatever it may be worth, is more than a political and social program. In the recent history of the church, the venerable institution has not had much luck synthesizing the emotional-subjective-mystical-paranormal and the love-justice-service sides of religion, but such a synthesis is biblically possible. When the church finds a creative and satisfying way to do it, it may suddenly become more relevant than it now strives to be, ministering to both the body and the spirit of man in wholeness and unity. ✕

The Search for a
Lost Paradise

After cutting, slicing, parsing, and dividing ideas and thoughts, the traditionally analytical Western world is turning eastward to discover how things can be put back together. Like Humpty Dumpty, we feel we are broken into a million fragments, and we hope that maybe some Eastern king and his horesmen might help us put ourselves back together, for we have a literally splitting spiritual headache.

I spoke to enough dedicated followers of the occult who moved along a certain path that I think one can outline the journey of a seeker working his way through the jumbled maze of the innumerable occult arts. One man's story, we'll call him Mr. K., is typical enough to give it to you in his words. Mr. K. is a hairdresser who owns an establishment that caters to a clientele that goes toward the upper end of the social/income scale:

"I heard about the occult from my clients even before it was the rage for everyone. I started with spiritualism, I suppose out of curiosity, but soon I felt I wanted this to lead me somewhere. I do not have an active religious affiliation and I guess what I was looking for was religion.

"Anyway, I stuck it out with spiritualism for a while. Then that seemed empty—you know, listening to people who wanted to talk with the dead can get boring after a while, and I didn't have that many friends yet who were on the other side, so I felt a little left out.

"I think though that the experience opened me up to the reality that is beyond us. I became intensely interested in the spiritual.

"My next bit was astrology, because I thought it might have some cosmic significance, but that didn't do much for what I sought. Some make it with the stars, but I didn't. I tried Tarot cards, *I Ching,* and some of the other things. They seemed terribly chancy, like the world was made up of fate and chance. I didn't find that did me any good.

"Right now, I think I have found what I have been looking for. I am studying Yoga, and in Eastern thought I have a glimmer at least of where I fit into the whole world-picture."

Mr. K. went from the occult to mysticism in an Eastern form. He sought a synthesis of reality and even the occult, in this day of analytical specialization, doesn't bring the whole picture together. Magic and witchcraft have potential for a harmonious view of the universe, but over the years of establishment hostility to their craft, these cults seem filled with a paranoid attitude and a marked lack of love. As Mr. K. journeyed through the dark recesses of the occult, he sought a healing that brought him into a new relationship with his fellowman, as well as a closing of his deeply felt wound between the universe and himself.

The occult makes it only so far with people: far enough to please the very egocentric, but not far enough to turn on the seeker after a comprehensive I-Thou, It-Me, synthesis.

There is a popular way to achieve at least the human interrelatedness side of this quest, an approach that has something more than a pseudoscientific ring about it. This is the encounter group. In these group sessions and sensitivity marathons, individuals overcome their logically and rationally induced inhibitions about emotions and learn to let go. They find new senses and awareness, new honesty and the power of emotion. Those who go to these groups regularly develop a kind of addiction to them. Everything is so real and honest inside the group, emotions are so free and open, that when they go into the workaday world they find it is so horribly artificial and phony they can't wait for the weekend when they get together with their group for another open heart session.

Another path toward overcoming the walls science has built around us, of freeing ourselves from the prison of intellect and going on to new heights on the emotions and feeling, is more dangerous: drugs. Hallucinogens such as LSD provide a host of paranormal experiences at the feeling level and a good trip allegedly takes you into a beautiful world that reality cannot duplicate.

The Christian mystic and the Eastern sage also offer a path to this unified, emotional vision of life. Their road involves hard work, intense discipline, powerful concentration. In a time of instant communication, frozen gourmet meals and headache remedies that go to work almost before they dissolve in your stomach, we lose patience with such arduous disciplines. In New York, where a number of authentic yogis hold classes, one teacher lamented, "The young people who come to me want everything so easy. They will not work. They want instant mysticism, and so I am afraid a number of my students go the drug route."

Beneath this quest, there lies a radical break with the scientific thought patterns that have dominated our world in recent times. One young man told me, "Oh, to hell with science. What has it brought us but trouble? We have atomic and hydrogen bombs, pollution, a raped landscape—all in the name of production and reason. Even our milk is full of radioactive fallout. The wonders of medicine, without birth control, have let the world get so overpopulated we may drown in a flood of humanity. And in the meantime, back at the ranch, everything is falling apart. Hate, violence—people who can't be human. No, we don't need science, but we do need humanity if we are going to survive."

This young man enjoyed all the economic benefits of science. He never knew want or starvation or illness without medical care. He benefited hugely from an economic order rationalized and managed for the goal of greatest productivity. He was the product of a technological society and, unlike the father who helped create that society, he was aware of the price in alienation and despair that technology extracts from its beneficiaries.

The Search for a Lost Paradise

What are the alternatives to the present system? That is the search of so many young people, and some of their parents too. The multiplicity of life-styles blossoming over the nation are examples of this intense search. Some find a commune dedicated to simplicity is the answer, others live in communes in urban centers that devote themselves to social activism. Some just plain drop out into a chemical world. Others grab onto those marvelously anti-rational, anti-establishment arts, the occult. A few find salvation in destruction—but common to all is a rejection of a totally "rational" society and the desire to find salvation through a new myth that respects humanity and human feeling.

There is a word for an emotional grab onto reality. It is trip. In one way or another, people try various trips. Some freak out, others get to a destination. Someday, all may go through the first station and the line and come to a common point. Then is when the New Religion—whatever it may be—will be born.

We might term the modern mood neo-Romanticism, after the movement in the late eighteenth and early nineteenth centuries that represented a reaction to the model of The Thinking Man put forth by exuberant rationalism. The early Romanticism denied the classical revival that preceded it, by emphasizing the imagination and emotions over pure intellect. *The Reader's Encyclopedia* gives a good summary of the romantic mood:

> The rise of romanticism was so gradual and it exhibited so many phases, some of them paradoxical, that a definition is nearly impossible. Broadly, romanticism might be said to involve the following characteristics: individualism; nature-worship; primitivism; an interest in medieval, Oriental, and vanished or alien cultures in general; philosophic idealism; a paradoxical tendency toward both free thought and religious mysticism; revolt against political authority and social convention; exaltation of physical passion; the cultivation of emotion and sensation for their own sakes; and a persistent attraction for the supernatural, the morbid, the melancholy, and the cruel.[1]

1. From *The Reader's Encyclopedia* (p. 871), compiled by William Rose Benet. Second Edition copyright © 1965 by Thomas Y. Crowell Company.

Though written of the original Romantic movement some one hundred years ago or more, it pretty well describes the mood of a large segment of the American population and explains the popularity of the occult.

Two German writers, drawing from the Romantic tradition, have become favorites of students today. One is Hermann Hesse, a Nobel Prize winning novelist. He is to today's youth what J. D. Salinger was to the generation of the fifties, the mirror for reflection and introspection. (One popular rock group took their name after his famous novel, *Steppenwolf*.) The other is Herbert Marcuse, an acutely intelligent philosopher of Marxist persuasion who provides the program for a robust, revolutionary romanticism. (More correctly, he doesn't provide a "program" for revolution; in fact, his recent decline in favor among some radicals stems from his assertion that the time is not ripe for a revolution—yet.)

In a provocative and perceptive essay, published in *The Yale Review,* Jeffrey Sammons points out the indebtedness of these men to Romanticism and emphasizes that underneath their thought lies buried the myth of a lost paradise:

> One comes upon it with great frequency in the German literature of the last two centuries; I think it is a kind of national neurosis that is related in some as yet undefined way to the perpetually disappointing conditions of German society, especially when they are seen in an idealistic perspective . . . "yearning" becomes the operative word of the artistic consciousness. Eventually, however, there is a tendency to locate the lost paradise just where the yearning was conceived in the first place. . . .
>
> What is remarkable is the extent to which semiconscious inheritances from the myth of the lost paradise permeate even the most radical German social criticism. . . . I cannot judge the extent to which Marxism itself may have been touched by the lost paradise myth, but the theory of alienation logically seems to suggest that at some (pre-industrial?) time, men had an organic relationship with the object world that has been destroyed and needs to be recovered. In Marcuse's case I do not doubt that the myth is present, and it accounts in substantial

part for the radicality of his denunciation of technological society.[2]

The modern quest for the lost paradise leads searchers to many places, and down some dangerous roads, but the common element in things as diverse as the occult, encounter groups, and drugs— if indeed there is a common element—may well be a desire to recover the purity of human feeling and relationship, the oneness that comes from an organic connection with the world of sense and suprasense, that anthropologists have told us is the state of primal man. In a future-oriented age, man seeks lost paradise in the prehistoric past; when science leads the path toward progress, the dissatisfied follow the trail into the past, after such ancient notions as the occult. Ironically, it may well be the progress of science that makes the recovery of tribal ways imperative. If Marshall McLuhan's speculation about our world becoming a global village, an organism connected by an instant electronic spinal cord, is correct, technology has provided the state and condition in which tribalism and unity of man can be achieved across broader geographical spaces than primitive tribalism allows.

I spoke with Dr. Perle Epstein, wife of a psychiatrist and a student of the occult. She was writing a book on witchcraft for children when we talked together. In her view, the craze for the occult stems from the way our logical faculties have been so conditioned that we frustrate our imaginative capacities.

"I was talking with a group of tenth-graders about my research," she explained. "I asked them how they felt about the occult. They were split. About half opposed it because it went contrary to reason, and others opposed it because it denied their orthodox faith. Some though were keen on ESP. In any case, I asked how many of them believed in elves and such things. Not a one responded. I know it sounds silly, but I am appalled that fourteen-year-olds today don't have the imagination to indulge in the unseen things.

"Imagination is one of the best things about the occult. It is anything you want it to be, a framework on which you can hang

2. Jeffrey Sammons, "Notes on the Germanization of American Youth," *The Yale Review* 59 (1970): 354–55, copyright Yale University.

any garments you wish. I got interested in it while doing my doctoral research at Columbia. I was working on the Cabala.

"People looking for higher truth aren't satisfied long with the occult as such. People with limited potential stick with it because it is a fad and they are led on by popularizers, but most move out of it eventually.

"I know people who have gone mad with the occult. You have to be healthy to take it. Pure occultism does hide you from the reality of life and lets you make immature responses to the world around you.

"The Cabala in Jewish history led to some disastrous results, yet beneath it was a desire for an immediate, personal encounter with God, something Judaism did not allow for. I personally think the Eastern religions have a clue for us. We in the West are very active, but don't know what we are active about. In the East, religion is more passive, more receptive to inner intuition. They have time to look for God within themselves. Zen monks when meditating have different EEG waves to specific stimuli; their meditation calms their minds in ways you can measure.

"It is true enough that Eastern passivity has bad consequences. They accept too much perhaps, and don't have that inner drive to correct injustice and right wrongs that we have. But somehow we have to blend Eastern and Western thought into a harmonious whole, because neither one has the whole answer and the way we are going now, the West is pulling itself apart at the seams."

How does a young person construct a faith that recovers a lost paradise? Some try total rejection of the existing structures, which religiously leads to magic and the long-rejected black arts. Others attempt a synthesis. A blend of various religious styles mixed together in combinations that would cause a scholar to wince is the current vogue among youth. One denominational press, supported by the most main-line of main-line Protestant groups, had a best seller recently which was described as a "potpourri of Zen, mysticism, Christianity, group therapy, awareness, Hinduism, Yoga, and some other spices to give it flavor." This lack of interest in logical analysis seems appropriate to a movement rejecting logic and, strangely, is probably more consistent with religious thought

In this engraving of Moses calling forth the plague of locusts upon the Pharaoh, taken from an edition of Luther's German Bible, the connection between the biblical events and magic is more obvious. As was customary among medieval artists, this engraver put Moses in contemporary dress and drew a German castle as the residence of the Pharaoh. Without knowing the source of this illustration, it looks like a magus exorcising demons from a nobleman's castle. What we call magic and what we call divine miracles seems to depend heavily upon the context.

than the carefully reasoned arguments of traditional theologians.

I interviewed a number of young people who were building their own religious views and I have a composite summary of what those who were working from a self-conscious Christian background were thinking:

"Christianity is too easy. You just accept it, and I can't buy that. I want more than to be saved; I want to grow.

"I think a lot of things may seem to be true, but as for bringing you closer to realizing yourself, they are not very relevant. I tried astrology, but I don't think much of it. It is like a way of defining yourself. I have friends who . . . well, like everything they do is written in the stars and they can explain it. But where does it lead them? I mean, if you define where the stars lead you but you don't like what you are doing, what good has it done? I want something that improves me, opens my potential.

"What led me on this search was really just the complete impossibility of believing what I have heard in church. No matter how much I studied it and no matter what I did, it just didn't turn me on. It was something taught, like any other subject, just presented to you as if it were the whole truth and you couldn't do anything about it.

"I also didn't like the idea of sin. It limits men, and I know that man for all his faults isn't that limited. He doesn't have to lean on God for everything, even though he needs God, but in a different relationship. More cooperation, more working together instead of having him hold all the marbles and you have nothing. Sin is a 'cultural' thing; you have to know what sin is to do sinning. Society sets up sin to keep itself together, because sin becomes breaking society's rules. I don't think it has much to do with communication with God when you get right down to it.

"But I am fascinated with life. My existence can't be started or stopped by some accident of physical birth or physical death.

"Life is a process and it must have a purpose. I am coming to believe in reincarnation. Origen, an early church father, had some of these ideas, but the church put him down. I am not sure I believe in it the way they do in the East, coming back for punishment and all that. But I believe in some way our existence goes on.

"When you affirm life as being most important, you realize you have a lot of potential and it seems that if you take a concept of God that allows you to develop yourself, work out your own soul, you have a God who really respects human beings.

"My idea of reincarnation, really, is a mental thing. Like, you grow in your understanding and awareness and with each step it is like a new insight, a new birth. It can change your life completely.

"The people who are aggressive, driven toward power and violence, are at the bottom of the spiritual ladder. They are only conscious of themselves, and they can't realize that you cannot turn another Self into a thing to use and manipulate. I think death will come to these people, because really they are dead already.

"Mysticism is a very personal thing. Once you institutionalize it, it is dead. Religion has to become institutionalized to survive, I guess, but the price is terrible. I hope for a religion that can be personal and free—and still survive."

Some of these ideas and visions of human potential come from drugs, LSD trips so lovely their participants want to create that same dream without artificial stimulants. Some come from the themes of youth today, their longing for love and cooperation and their rejection of established institutions.

Three ideas permeate these various viewpoints on the value of the occult: emotionalism, personal striving, and anti-institutionalism. All three reflect egocentricity. It would seem that the church as it now exists is going to lose on all counts, but this is not necessarily so.

The present gospel proclaimed in the church is very much other-centered. Taking its clues from the cross symbol, in which Christ gave himself away, it calls man to empty himself for his brother. Of course, not many in the pews follow this advice, perhaps for the simple reason that they aren't Christ—the option offered, in other words, is rather unrealistic from a human point of view. The movement toward human potential, that is beginning to dominate psychology at this time, does not deny man's responsibility to his fellows, but it insists that unless a person is whole and complete, he is giving away nothing. Unless you are somebody first you have nothing to offer. In its zeal to proclaim the ethical imperatives of

Christianity, the church overlooks the need of people for inner cultivation. Few members of the main-line denominations speak openly of their religious experiences—because most of them haven't had any—but youth on the fringes of traditional society willingly talk at length about their spiritual journeys.

When theocentricity denies the worth of man, it loses its moorings in the harbor of religion, which is man himself. God, after all, doesn't need religion; the whole spiritual enterprise is for the benefit of human beings.

Important biblical happenings often are accompanied by paranormal events, such as the thunder and lightning which announced the Decalogue.

Emotionalism also bothers the respectable churches. A few have noted that the fastest growing churches in the country are those that stress personal religious experience—the evangelistic sects and the pentecostal groups. As Harvey Cox once quipped, a Southern Baptist is basically a "head" because when he goes to church, he can have a trip. It may be a bad trip, but it can be a good trip as well. Neither possibility is open in the formal worship of sedate churches, with their cool, remote God and their call to right decisions and proper living. The transcendent God can become too remote in his holy place, to the point where men lose touch with him. Pietism, which is an emotionalized form of Protestant mysticism, degenerated into legalistic and life-denying nitpicking. Few took up the Quaker notion of the inner light, and this leaves an emotional void that desperately needs filling. Some church groups turn to group process, with a thin veneer of religion applied overlaid on a mass of psychology, to help fill this vacuum, but it would seem that religion in and of itself might accomplish the emotional expectations of people as they seek a new perception of the world.

The church generally attacks personal striving, at least among Protestants who affirm the "grace alone, faith alone" concept of salvation. If Christianity must have some hard-core if unalterable propositional truth that people must simply accept as part of joining this path to trusting God, there is still room for personal efforts in terms of spiritual discipline. But, as William Rauscher said, this kind of spirituality is long gone from many churches. It is interesting to read in one of Arthur Ford's books a chapter on uncovering your psychic powers, which is really a fine manual on meditative techniques that enhance spirituality and closeness to God without denying the body or failing to affirm the worth of human life. The fact that this type of teaching can be found in occult literature may explain why people turn to these fields. The church fought many battles against gnosticism which, apart from its unusual and difficult philosophical basis that ran contrary to Christian doctrine, cultivated an I-am-more-holy-than-thou attitude. Certainly this danger exists; it is what finally made pietism the sterile dead end it became. But perhaps we have learned something over the years, and can discover a way to incorporate personal spiritual discipline into a healthy Christian outlook. Theologically, the trick here is to find some formulation which doesn't deny sin to the extent that man doesn't need God's grace, but at the same time allows for some confidence in man's ability to grow in grace. The Greek Orthodox theory that asserts that when Christ became incarnate in humanity he changed the quality of the whole human race may provide the beginning of such a theology for Western Christianity. Tolerating striving implies allowing people to play a bit with doctrine; this approach doesn't work with an intellectual orthodoxy.

The anti-institutional element is hard for traditional churches to cope with because they are the paragons of the Establishment.

However, there are encouraging signs that some churches manage to embrace fringe groups not totally within the institutional fabric. Perhaps institutionalism is a necessary evil; probably so, but the institutions need not be sterile.

There are ample resources in the Christian faith to affirm life and human potential. Christ died that we might live. As one church father put it, God became man that man might become God. If the work of Christ means anything, it must enhance human life and release its fullest potential.

Christian mysticism has, over the years, striven to provide a sense of oneness with God and with man through spiritual growth. In the course of its history, mysticism has had its aberrations and excesses, even as the occult has gone off the edge of sanity. But this doesn't necessarily condemn the idea because religious experience, like the occult, is pretty much what you bring to it. Bring neurosis and, in Freud's words, "repressed anal instincts" and you are in for a bad trip either way. Should the church for any reason find it too difficult to look backwards to its own mystical heritage, it can generously and ecumenically turn eastward and learn from the sages there. Christianity, as we often overlook, is an Eastern religion shoved by history into a set of Western clothes.

In his classic series of Bampton Lectures given at the turn of the century, William Inge spoke of Christian mysticism in words that ring with the sounds of the contemporary quest:

> In necromancy, astrology, alchemy, palmistry, table-turning, and other delusions, we have what some count the essence, and others the reproach, of Mysticism. But these are, strictly speaking, scientific and not religious errors. From the standpoint of religion and philosophy, the important change is that, in the belief of these later mystics, the natural and the spiritual are, somehow or other, to be reconciled; the external world is no longer regarded as a place of exile from God, or a delusive appearance; it is the living vesture of the Diety; and its "discordant harmony," though "for the many it needs interpreters," yet "has a voice for the wise" which speaks of things behind the veil. The glory of God is no longer figured as a blinding white light in which all colors are combined and lost; but is seen as a

"many-colored wisdom," which shines everywhere, its varied hues appearing not only in the sanctuary of the lonely soul, but in all the wonders that science can discover, and all the beauties that art can interpret. Dualism, with the harsh asceticism which belongs to it, has given way to a brighter and more hopeful philosophy; men's outlook upon the world is more intelligent, more trustful, and more genial; only for those who perversely seek to impose the ethics of selfish individualism upon a world which obeys no such law, science has in reserve a blacker pessimism than ever brooded over the ascetic of the cloister.[3]

The mantle of mysticism has been picked up in more recent times by the French scientist and Jesuit theologian, Teilhard de Chardin. His books received a favorable reception, especially by scientific people. He did for the bridging of the gap between science and theology what his contemporary Paul Tillich did for the chasm between philosophy and religion. He has the vision of man evolving spiritually as well as biologically. Man is developing in close harmony with God, and is moving toward what he calls the omega-point, or the fullness of Christ. From his writings may emerge the viable theology of the future, one which satisfies the complex mystical strivings of men in the present time. Psychic groups such as Spiritual Frontiers Fellowship band together religious people searching for a recovery of the mystical experience.

Mysticism must not be confused with emotion as such. Mysticism is a perception of reality; it is not the way everyone is able (or should be able) to embrace reality, but it is a means of perception which must be honored as authentic. W. T. Stace in *Mysticism and Philosophy* describes seven psychological characteristics of the mystical perception: as to perception—unity, timelessness, objective reality, and the divine; as to feeling—blessedness, joy/peace, a sense that words can't convey the experiences, and a tendency to use paradoxes in expressing truth.

The essentially *non*rational (as distinguished from *ir*rational) mysticism can exist with and enhance rational theology. Professor Walter Clark observes: "Our religion needs color, vitality, energy,

3. William Inge, *Christian Mysticism* (Cleveland: World Publishing Co., 1958), pp. 299–300.

and meaning if it is to stay alive. This comes from ecstasy, of which mystical perceptions are simply the deepest, most satisfying, and the most cogent forms. But just as rational religion needs the leaven, the salt of the ecstatic, so ecstasy can get out of hand to become the fanatical or the mindlessly emotional. The mystic needs his reason to supply critical balance and direction in order to save him from excess. We can think of the hippies, probably the most dynamically religious sector in our society at the moment. But the lives of the hippies too often lack structure. The hippies need the church as much as the churches need the hippies."[4]

Of course, the church has the option of casting the red cloak of the Devil upon the occult. Or it can honestly look at itself and recover once again some of the elements in its tradition which, under the pressures of rationalism, it has relegated to the closet. The avant-garde faith of today may well be one which goes back to its original source, as most religious reformations have done.

One point is obvious: The church is becoming profoundly un-spiritual, even a little ashamed of religion as such. The occult craze ought to tell the ecclesiastical powers that even though their institutions are in trouble, religion as such is once again in the mainstream. Then the church can begin to recover its paranormal, its mystical, its purely spiritual perception of reality without shame or embarrassment. It, too, can loosen up and take a trip with its people. A number of people are obviously waiting for such a move. If Christ is what the church proclaims him to be—the sum of all creation, the Lord of heavens and earth—surely he is *the* focal point for man's spiritual quest. An immediate encounter with God, a mystical sense of oneness with all humanity, a cosmic Christ who embraces all creation, may, if the mystics are correct, lead to the cooperation and peace among men which so far the hard ethical sermons have failed to produce.

Paradise lost may one day be regained. ∨℘

4. Walter Clark, "Mysticism in the Religious Life," *Spiritual Frontiers* 2 (1970): 210.